Gateway to the Dead

A Ghost Hunter's Field Guide

Gateway to the Dead: A Ghost Hunter's Field Guide
Second Edition

First Edition published as *The Ghost Hunter's Field Guide, 2010*

Nocturna Press
www.NocturnaPress.com

ISBN-13: 978-0-9854314-3-3

Cover design by Nocturna Press
Front cover image by Frozenstarro/Cemetery Gate/Fotolia.com
Interior images used with permission

Acknowledgements

Dedicated to my mother, aunt, grandmothers, grandfathers, and White Cloud, who all communicate with me from the other side, and who encouraged me to write this book.

Table of Contents

Introduction.. 7

Chapter 1 What are Ghosts?...................................... 11

Chapter 2 Contacting Spirits.................................... 19

Chapter 3 Descriptions of Non-Physical Entities :
The Lecher, Time Imprint, Aliens, Poltergeist, Demons, Orbs, Fog, and Apparitions, Plasma, Ball Lightning, Spirit Fog, Tree Sprites, Fairies, Shadow People.. 25

Chapter 4 How to Communicate With Ghosts:
Margie's Meditation Method, Other Ways to Raise Your Level of Consciousness and Vibratory Rate, How to Communicate With Ghosts Using Your Sixth Sense.. 43

Chapter 5 Ghost Hunting Tools and Techniques:
Laser Thermometer, Digital Thermometer, EMF Detector, Digital Cameras and Video, Motion-Activated Cameras, Night Vision, Digital Recorders, Wind Meter, Pendulums and Dowsing Rods, UV Light, Psychics, White Noise, How to Make Your Own Ghost Communicator, Wind or Fan, Drinking Glass, Other Devices, Your Ghost Hunting Kit.... 59

Chapter 6 How to Dowse for Spirits:
How to use dowsing equipment, How to make your own dowsing rod, How to make your own clay pendulum.................................. 67

Chapter 7 Photographing Ghosts:
How to Photograph Ghosts, Photos of anomalous objects................ 73

Chapter 8 Good Places to Find Ghosts 83

Chapter 9 The Investigation Process
Interviewing Witnesses, Interview Form, Ruling out Other Possibilities, How to Get Rid of Ghosts... 85

Chapter 10 How to Protect Yourself While Ghost Hunting:
White Light, Crystals, Encounters with Negative Entities................... 99

Table of Contents

Chapter 11 Real Ghost Hunts:
Ghost Hunt Experiences, Haunted Chimneys........................... 109

Chapter 12 Famous Haunted Sites to Visit..................... 199

Chapter 13 Paranormal Radio and TV Shows.................. 225

Chapter 14 Resources... 229

Chapter 15 Glossary of Paranormal Terms..................... 231

Bibliography.. 244

About the Author.. 248

Introduction

I was raised in the Kansas City area by my father, who was a salesman for Encyclopedia Britannica; and my mother, who was a housewife. Mom had a bachelor's degree in business, but she felt it was important to stay home with me and my younger sister and brother, and at that time most mothers didn't work anyway.

Mom was largely responsible for seeing that I succeeded in school. Both of my parents were very intelligent, but my father has a genius level IQ, as did his father and two grandfathers. This may explain why he understood my growing abilities as a psychic, although he didn't discuss this with me during my childhood. He has since spent much time studying and becoming a proficient healer and psychic.

Neither of my parents ever told me to stop seeing things, or had any fears about my abilities as many people do. The open-mindedness of both of my parents likely allowed me to open myself up to more experiences.

I remember seeing energy fields around trees at the age of five; and by age eleven I could see and talk to ghosts, see future events, and communicate with my cat telepathically. At first, all of this was a little frightening. But after a few years I got used to it, and I realized that ghosts found me because I could see and talk to them while others did not. In school, however, I was very shy and kept to myself because I was afraid of what others might say if they found out what I could do.

I developed an interest in the paranormal, and borrowed lots of books from the library to study. I was also curious about UFOs, although at the time I didn't realize that I'd actually had contact with

UFOs. I wouldn't find out until years later, under hypnosis, that UFO contact began when I was sixteen months old and continued throughout my life. I mention this because I feel that the UFO contact is responsible for much of my clairvoyant abilities since after each significant UFO encounter, my abilities seemed to increase.

My mother bought me a book about Edgar Cayce when I was fifteen. This was my first exposure to others who had similar experiences to mine. Once in a while Dad bought me a UFO magazine to read. Although neither of my parents knew how to help me—since they had no personal experience with clairvoyance, clairaudience, telepathy, and clairsentience—they didn't hesitate to get materials that I could use for research.

While I was a sophomore in high school, my science teacher introduced extra sensory perception to the class. I was thrilled that he had an interest in the subject, but didn't mention my own experiences with ESP. The teacher tested everyone in the class using the famous *Rener* cards that include a square, circle, wavy lines, even cross, and a star. I did very well and he insisted on doing more testing with me after class. This turned into a three-month long experiment every afternoon after school with the teacher and two other students. They tested me with a fifty-two-card deck, numbers, letters, and anything they could think of; which included asking me to try to foretell future events and diagnose illness.

At the same time the testing was going on I started to see ghosts in my house. I already knew there were spirits there because I could feel their presence, and one had appeared to four of us the first day we moved in. But this was different. There were many three-dimensional faces in the walls of the hallway and bathroom that moved and spoke, although I could not hear what they said. We also experienced footsteps, doors banging, and lights going off and on by themselves. My cat, whiskers, would sometimes look at some invisible thing on the ceiling or wall then run out of the room.

I gradually became more sensitive to spirits, and one day watched a scene from the past unfold before me in my bedroom. A woman, dressed in an 1880s style black dress and wide brimmed hat, killed a younger woman with a butcher knife. I could see the younger woman screaming, but again, heard no sound along with it. This was especially disturbing, and I thought I'd lost my mind, but my science teacher recommended that we research our house.

I found that the house had been built in the 1850s and was a doctor's hospital in the later part of the century. There had been several mysterious deaths in the house during the time that the doctor owned it. Coincidentally, the mansion just two doors down had a dark history to it as well, so it is no wonder that the area was active with spirits.

By the time I reached twenty-one years of age, I'd started giving psychic readings for people. I answered their questions, looked into their futures, and checked for medical issues they should be aware of. The readings helped to supplement my income from my job as a professional musician. By practicing on hundreds of people, I got better and better. However, I soon found out that when you are an open channel you might unknowingly allow some dark entities to enter your life. So, I had to learn how to protect myself from these forces.

At age twenty-two, I got my first official missing persons case with a private investigator. He was working on a case in Kansas. I was able to find the location of the kidnapper, find out why they did it, discover who else was involved, and see when the best time would be for them to go in to rescue the child. After the child was found, I received a call from the child's aunt. She told me the child was found physically unharmed and wanted to thank me.

Apparently, if they hadn't arrived when they did, the girl would have been going into a white slavery ring the next day. After that, I decided that I needed to work with law enforcement and private investigators, which I continue to this day. I don't charge for finding missing persons, and am happy to help anyone who asks, if I can.

Ghost hunting is now more than a serious hobby for me, and that is why I founded the non-profit association Quest Investigation Group. QUEST is comprised of a team of investigators trained in forensics investigation and intuitive investigation. Our team does ghost hunting at the request of homeowners or building owners in an effort to gain scientific evidence of ghosts and other entities, and to improve communication with those who have traveled to the other side. Sometimes I talk about these investigations on my radio show Un-X News. Visit UnXnews.com for more information.

I have had good luck working with a team of people, and I suggest the same for others working in the field. This book approaches the subject of ghost hunting in a slightly different manner that normal, using not only scientific tools to capture evidence, but also the use of the sixth sense in locating, communicating, and gaining information about spirits.

I hope you find this book interesting and useful in your own ghost hunting endeavors.

Margie Kay

CHAPTER 1

What are Ghosts?

Just what are ghosts, spirits, or apparitions? I have some opinions based on my years of research on the subject and experience in contacting people who have passed on. Since I can usually readily communicate with the spirit of a deceased person, and they often answer questions that only that person's family would know, it is obvious that I am really speaking to the true spirit of that person. In case you are worried about a "false spirit" coming through, we have methods of protection against that sort of thing; and we always use them before any communication. You'll find more on that topic later in this book.

In some rare cases where I can't speak to the spirit directly, I will get the "essence" of the person and know what their personality was and what their answer might be. This might sound very odd, but the only way I can explain it is that I know what they would say if they were here.

I have also had encounters with other entities besides ghosts—including aliens, orbs, rods, poltergeists, tiny white lights, fairies or angels, and strange, unexplainable creatures. I believe that these types of beings exist in a higher dimension and are able to come to our third/fourth dimension at certain times to do whatever it is they wish. It is clear that they are observing living humans much of the time. What is not so clear is exactly what they are and why they are observing us. All I know is that I sense that they are all here for a reason and that even though we may not yet have the capability of understanding them, they do exist.

I see the vibratory rate or energy field of living beings. This field is in and around the body and aura and looks like layers of energy just above the skin or surface, then extends to about three feet out in all directions. It vibrates or shakes. All living things and metals, rocks, etc. have an electromagnetic energy field, which is measurable. Most humans emit approximately seven volts of electricity, which can be detected with a volt meter, therefore, have an electromagnetic field as well.

Spirits probably have a much higher vibration than living people. I believe that each dimension has a range of vibration and that beings that are in tune with that dimension call that space their home and exist in it. For instance, we, in our physical bodies, may not be able to move to another dimension even if we wanted to. But take us out of that body: in the astral body if alive, or in spirit form if dead, and we can easily move through our third (physical) and fourth (time) dimensions we are familiar with, as well as the fifth dimension.

Take a look at the electromagnetic spectrum on the next page and you'll see what I'm talking about. There are measurable radio waves, cosmic waves, visible color spectrum, etc. that our scientists have determined have different lengths of waves or vibration. I suspect that just above the visible light spectrum is the next dimension up—the fifth—just a little further up the scale than normal perceptions will allow. Psychics may more easily see this level because they vibrate at a higher rate and are more in tune with that level.

As an example of how "tuning" works, if you put a stringed instrument in a place by itself, and then play another stringed instrument of the same type in the same room, the first instrument will sound by itself. Try playing the A string on a violin and then listen to the other violin and you'll hear it sound. This is similar to a

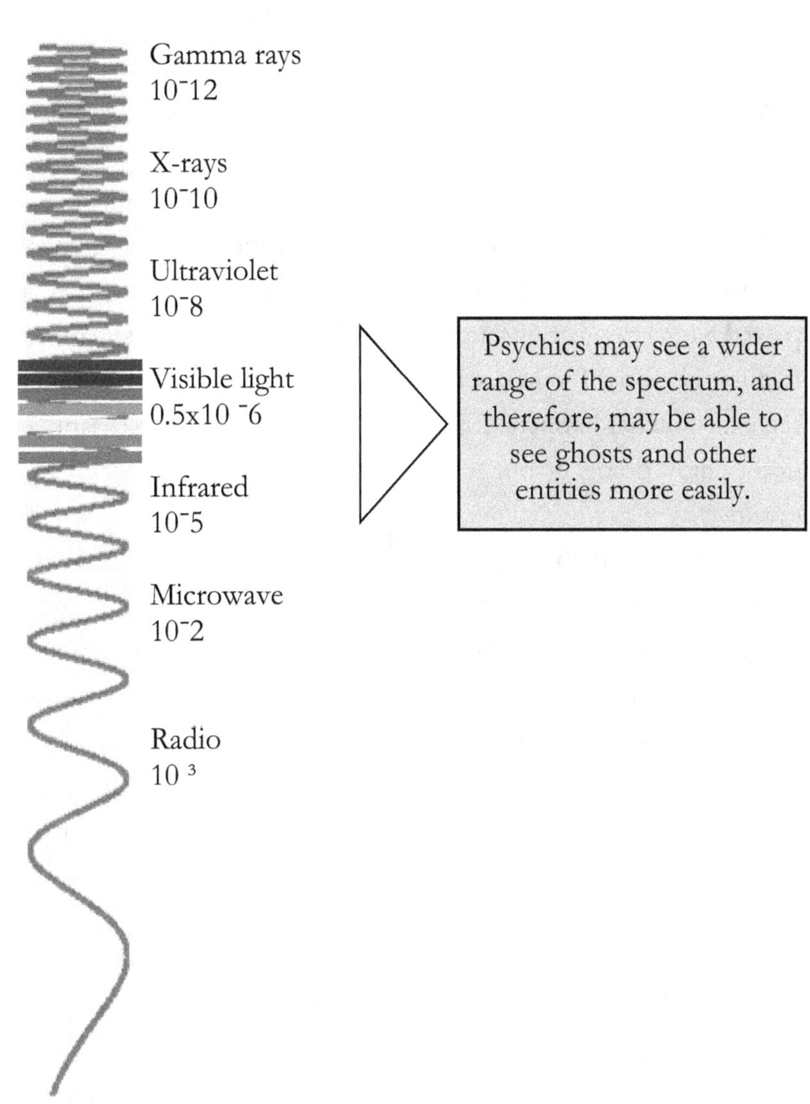

The Electromagnetic Spectrum

psychic tuning in to a vibration of similar rate or value.

Another explanation for apparitions may be what I call a *Time Imprint.* Other investigators have come to this conclusion as well. I base this on the fact that some "ghosts" look like they are going about their daily activities and are completely unaware of the observer. There is no communication with the observer whatsoever and the observer cannot get a reaction from the "ghost." Most paranormal investigators believe that some buildings, perhaps because of the materials used in construction, record events that are played back later just like a movie. In fact, in some investigations for missing persons, I watch what looks like a movie of the scene and see exactly what happened. Most of the time it is not pleasant, and I don't enjoy doing it, but it is a way to determine the sequence of events.

So how is it that some of us see ghosts and some do not? I believe it has something to do with genetics and practice. Genetically, some of us may inherit genes from our ancestors that allow us to use our sixth sense (and seventh and so on) more readily than other people. Just as someone may be predisposed to be a great golfer, another might be naturally very psychic. Since my own family is now three generations of psychics, and I know many other psychic families as well, this is strong evidence to support the theory of genetics having something to do with the sixth sense.

Practice also has a great deal to do with the ability to communicate with the other side. Children are more open about these subjects than adults. The child has not yet been told that he can't see these things or that they are not really there, so he does not know that he shouldn't see them. If the child is allowed to grow up without prejudice about whether or not something such as a ghost does exist—he will learn to accept and communicate with the other side and may also remember past lives. This may also be the source of imaginary friends. This knowledge can be a great benefit emotionally because we have confirmation that our ancestors really do look out for us, as is evidenced by the many people who are saved from harm by their loved ones who have passed on. You may feel better now knowing that you don't need to feel the sense of loss so badly when someone passes over, and that you will live on as well.

There have been numerous occasions where a spirit helped me or other members of our family. In August of 2006 my youngest daughter had an emergency C-section to save her baby. The baby was just under thirty-two weeks gestation. For some reason, she came to work forty-five minutes early that day, and it was a good thing because we were able to rush her to the hospital immediately. The baby was less than four pounds and had to remain in a neonatal care unit for six weeks. During that time, he contracted a staph infection from a catheter in his arm that was used to deliver food and medication directly to the blood.

The baby was thriving and doing well for about two weeks, then he started to lose weight. This was not a good sign, and the doctors and nurses could not figure it out. One day, a nurse suddenly got the idea to do a test for staph, even though she thought it would be remote possibility. The result was positive. Fast treatment with antibiotics worked and the baby got well quickly. If it had gone on further without treatment he might not have survived.

My mother died the month before this occurred, and I was surprisingly in communication with her right away. She told me that she mentioned the staph test to the nurse so she would act on it. We believed it.

Other examples of this have occurred as warnings of future events. One day I heard the voice of my grandfather while I was driving in my car. He said "Take another street" and I immediately turned to take another route. I later found out there was a big accident on the street I normally travel on.

Another communication from the other side occurred when I was seventeen years old. My mother was driving with me in the front seat and my thirteen-year-old brother was in the back seat. A sudden ice storm came up as we drove north on 71 Highway from Springfield to Kansas City, and produced black ice on the road. I suddenly saw golden light around me and heard my grandfather's voice say "put on your seat belts." My grandfather had been dead for several years.

This was during a time when no one wore seat belts. I told my mother and brother to buckle up as I hooked up my seatbelt. Not five minutes later, my mother lost control of the car on the ice and we spun around, then headed towards a big drop-off. There was only a guardrail between us and the cliff. We were gong so fast that I thought surely we would go over the railing, but we didn't. We all came out of the accident with minor injuries, except for my mother's broken nose. If we hadn't had our seatbelts on, it surely would have been worse.

In 1976, my sister, Alice, went on a trip to Colorado with her best friend and her family over the week of July 4th. She was sixteen at the time. The group was getting ready to go out and Alice was fixing her hair when an apparition of my deceased grandfather suddenly appeared in the mirror. Alice turned around, but the vision disappeared. She knew something was wrong and called home, but couldn't get anyone to answer the phone. She was panicked. Later that night I was awakened at four o'clock in the morning by my grandfather's voice saying, 'contact your mother'. I also knew something was wrong.

At that time I was living in Carrollton, Missouri in a tiny

apartment with my new husband and no phone, so called the next day and could not get an answer. It was a few days before we found out that there had been a house fire on July 4th caused by kids shooting bottle rockets at the wood shingled roof. My mother, grandmother, and brother had all been moved to a temporary apartment, and were all okay.

I am in almost constant contact now with both my grandfathers, grandmothers, my mother, and a spirit named White Cloud, who was a Native American in this area. White Cloud says I was a member of his tribe in a former life many centuries ago and was a healer and shaman named "Medicine Woman." All of my guides give me advice and assistance on different issues and help with cases I work on.

My grandfather Lombardo told me that he sits on a council of thirteen members who are guardians for a large group of people. He is the guardian of our family as well, which makes sense because that is what he did in life. We are a large Italian family (on my mother's side), and all who remember him say my grandfather was the token "godfather" of the family and made sure everyone was taken care of. Whenever there is something that could cause potential harm to a family member, even to his great-grandchildren that he never met, grandfather Lombardo gives us a warning by appearing to us.

The contact I have with all of my guides is similar to speaking one-on-one with a person as if they were physically in the room with me, but we communicate telepathically. I hear their voices clearly and just to test myself at times—I have someone else ask something I could not possibly know about and my guides give me the answer.

Sometimes I'll ask for some piece of information that only the person I'm working with and the spirit could know about, and they never fail to either show or tell me something unique. This is usually the way I'll start a communication in order to make sure that I'm talking to the right person. The spirit will give me details such as their favorite eye shadow color, or what is in the wallet that now belongs to their son.

Talking with ghosts is how I got interested in hauntings and ghost hunting. As a researcher, I am looking for proof of the existence of spirits, which is in turn, proof that we all live on even after death of the body.

CHAPTER 2

Contacting Spirits

During trance state, I contact spirits and have a conversations with them, just like I would with a living person. I have learned how to put myself in a light trance state without the assistance of a hypnotist, and this is very helpful when contacting those who have passed over. The answers are offered telepathically, which I hear as regular voices. The spirits tell me they are not "dead," but that they are most assuredly alive and in fact, are more alive in spirit than when they are in a human body. They say that they felt trapped while in a human body, but when in spirit form feel very free. I'd like to share a conversation with you that I had with my mother shortly after her death, which explains a lot about the spirit world.

Contact with Marie Lombardo

August 11, 2006 | 11:30 p.m.

I was meditating while sitting in the hot tub on our porch when Mom popped into my head. Since my brother, Frank, and I had told her we would try to contact her on the eleventh of every month, I shouldn't have been surprised to see her appear but was, nonetheless. She asked if I wanted to know anything, and I said, yes, there were some things I'd like to know about the afterlife that I'd like to hear from her directly. I asked what kind of a body the spirit was made of and how it traveled around. She told me some very remarkable things:

What it's Like on the Other Side

A: The spirit body is made of light photons and pure energy. It is a very subtle body, yet it does have measurable mass. This body usually travels as a ball of light—you have seen them as orbs– because it is easier that way. Then when the spirit arrives at its destination it can form into whatever shape it desires, in the case of someone who recently passed he/she would appear to the person as that old body so he will be recognized. But the spirit body can form into whatever it wants, and in fact, can be in multiple locations at the same time. It can even choose to incarnate in the body of an animal or plant, or even other beings on other planets if it desires.

Q: Wow. Can you, say, visit with two people at once?

A: Yes, absolutely. And in different times.

Q: In different times?

A: Well, time as you know it. There is no time where I am. But I can appear to you at my age of 10 or 75 if I wish—whatever might be appropriate. You have experienced this yourself when talking to mother and dad (she means her mother and father) and have seen them at different ages.

The choice to live in a particular living physical body is up to the spirit – the choice having to do with what the spirit needs to experience in order to grow, or even just to have an experience to know about it. It doesn't always have to do with growth of the soul. The spirit can split up into many parts and have several lifetime experiences all at once. This is why some people have dreams or visions of other locations and families that they feel are familiar to them—or Déjà vu. Part of the soul had that experience and brought it home to the rest of itself. You may have seen balls of light at some time and then saw that appeared to split into several smaller orbs. This is the same soul—just different parts of it.

There is also something you should know about death. The soul is more at home in its spirit body without the encumbrance of a physical body, and so in a manner of speaking "death" might mean just the opposite to a spirit. In other words, it is somewhat of a death to be in a living, physical body that is very restrictive. The soul body can move about at will, has no health problems, does not need to eat as you know it (we get fuel from the essence of plants), and can pretty much do what it wants. In fact, I can visit all of my relatives that passed over before me, all of my living relatives, and whoever else I want to visit at any time. I can also travel anywhere on the planet and to any other planet. Somewhat like what you know as Astral Travel.

The astral body moves around in a similar fashion to the soul body and this is another method of communicating with those on this side. You have done this but don't use it as often as trance work. It is different in that the astral body not only sees everything around it like you do in trance, but it is clearer and you can physically touch and feel things, too.

This conversation was quite incredible and really helped me understand "death" better. I am no longer as afraid to cross over and when the time comes I am sure it will be very pleasant. I hope that this will help people have a greater understanding of death of the body.

During my trance sessions I've gathered a lot of information from my ancestors and guides about what it is like in the spirit world. Some of what they've told me is pretty amazing and they've been insistent that I write this information down and share it with as many people as possible. Following is a list of things my guides would like everyone to know:

- When the body dies you will feel light, happy and free with no pain or discomfort. If you had a painful illness or injury in life you'll be very relieved not to be in that body any more. There is always someone waiting for you in spirit when you leave your body. That person is most likely someone you knew in life – like a trusted family member. They may be accompanied by other family members and there may be a spirit guide there you'll recognize as your guardian. These entities will tell you what to expect and help you through the transition. You'll be taken through the lifetime you just left from birth to death doing a life review. You'll be able to see all of the good and bad things you did to help the progress of your soul. Then you'll get to watch your funeral and spend time with family members. Some family and friends may be aware of your presence.

- Soon you will learn how to travel around. You are a tiny ball of light photons with electrical energy now. You can move from place to place very quickly in this form. You may change your form to something more familiar if you wish, but this is not necessary. If you are able to communicate with the living, you may learn how to take energy from batteries or other energy sources in order to form a recognizable shape, but this method usually takes some time to perfect. Spirits readily communicate with each other and with trance mediums. Spirits may witness astral travelers or aliens passing by as well. Aliens don't inhabit this plane, but they pass through it to get to and from Earth.

- Ghosts/Spirits retain their personality when they pass over. This is why there are both "good" and "bad" ghosts – if they were bad in life, they'll usually still be bad in death and vice-versa. There is no automatic awakening or raising of consciousness at the moment of death, and I've been told that there is no heaven or hell as usually described by some religions. This is something your guides will explain. There are however, multiple dimensions, and as the consciousness is raised the spirit will be able to inhabit those realms. The spirit works with guides through many lifetimes and periods in-between lifetimes in spirit to work on raising its vibrations in order to experience the higher realms.

- Your soul is the part of you that is always alive and can never die. The earthly body is just a temporary body for the spirit to inhabit, and that is the only part that dies at death. The spirit recognizes this and remembers it at the time of death. The concept of reincarnation used to be taught in all of the world's religions but has been removed from some religious teachings in order to instill fear and make people behave a certain way.

- You may decide to stay in spirit or to reincarnate on the earth or somewhere else in the Universe. Most people from Earth reincarnate on Earth because it is familiar. They also reincarnate as humans in the same family groups since they feel comfortable with those other spirits. Often family members will have experiences as each other's children, siblings, spouses, parents, and grandparents. However, if a person wanted he/she could reincarnate as an animal or even a plant or rock, depending on the type of experience needed or desired. This usually does not happen until the person has raised his vibratory rate to a certain level.

- Spirits can incarnate on other planets as well as our own. If coming here directly from another planet, a person may feel like he doesn't belong here and feel out of place- like he doesn't "fit in." It make take several generations for this feeling to go away. This is why a lot of recently incarnated spirits often look at the stars a night and have a sense of not belonging here, but rather "somewhere else."

CHAPTER 3

Descriptions of Non-Physical Entities

People often ask me what the different types of entities are that we encounter during investigations. There are quite a few, and I'll list some of the more common ones here for your reference.

The Lecher

Among the non-physical entities are some who mean us no harm, but that get their life force by taking energy from humans. They may attach themselves to a person, which can cause extreme fatigue for the host. I had one of these attached to me in 1985, and it was removed by another psychic who asked the entity to move on to something else like a cow or sheep, which happened to be nearby. She saw the entity as a black shadowy shape attached to my right side. After the entity was gone, I felt immediately better and no longer was so fatigued. When this type of entity is removed the person usually feels much better because their energy is no longer being drained. These types of beings seldom return.

Time Imprint

A time imprint is simply a recorded "movie" of events that plays over an over again. There is no spirit present, you are just seeing the movie play. Most ghost hunters suspect that the materials used in buildings such as plaster, nails, and paint somehow record events in a similar fashion to the way film does. The way to tell if this is indeed what you are seeing is if the "ghost" does not appear to see you or interact with you or anyone else in the room while you are there. Another indication is if the same exact scene plays itself over and over again. Time Imprints can be useful when trying to solve unanswered questions about events. Time Imprints are typically associated with someone doing the same routine over and over again in the same location, such as one case where every time a woman brushed her teeth before retiring she saw the reflection of a man walk behind her from the doorway towards the shower.

Poltergeists

A Poltergeist may or may not be an entity of a person who lived on the earth. Activity such as moving objects, pushing, objects thrown across the room, objects missing and sometimes found in other locations, banging in or on the walls, furniture being rearranged, etc. has been attributed to a person in the house who is going through an emotional time. It is most common when teenagers, especially girls, are living in the home. Teens are usually not aware that they are causing this activity, and it will normally pass after the child gets older. If the teenager phenomena has been ruled out, then it is time to look at other possible sources.

Remember the movie "*Poltergeist*"? This is a true (but embellished for the movies) story about a family who experienced extremely violent phenomenon in their home, and found out later that they were living on a Native American burial ground. The ground was likely protected by spirits assigned to the area by the Native Americans long ago. It is best to thoroughly check out a location first before buying a house to avoid trouble like this!

I did a poltergeist investigation in Kansas City in 1993 along with several other experienced mediums. We were requested to do a clearing for a woman who had nightly activity in her house. The spirit moved and broke dishes, glasses and other objects, threw things across the room, slammed doors, and stomped around the house. He appeared as a black shadowy human figure and walked through doors and walls. The homeowner reported hearing audible moaning sounds as well. This was getting out of hand and the owner needed help.

Upon arrival at the house, I found three psychics in the living room who were scared stiff and refused to assist us. They sensed a very powerful, negative spirit and were unable to confront it. Another medium and I scanned the entire house, and both of us were drawn to the front bedroom as the main location of the spirit. I went into a trance and saw a well underneath the bedroom that went many feet down. I saw the body of a man in the well. The man had been murdered. He wanted resolution and felt wronged, and was very angry about it.

The sprit of the man gained power from the people living in the house due to their fear of him, and also from a Native American spirit protector of the area. Perhaps the well I saw was a natural well cut into the stone many thousands of years ago.

The murder happened in the mid 1800s so the killer was long dead. After I explained this to the man he calmed down and a few minutes later the six of us (five mediums and the homeowner) saw a white ball of light about three feet in diameter move from the bedroom, through the living room and through three of us, and then out the far wall. We felt this entity move through us and all of us got cold chills. The homeowner reported back to us that she had no more activity in the house after that. In my experience, there may be other non-human entities that cause poltergeist activity, but they are rare.

Demons

There are exorcists and demonologists who specialize in dealing with demons. I don't. On one occasion, I saw three small creepy looking creatures that might be described as demons, but in fact, I don't know for sure what they were. They could easily have taken on a devilish appearance for effect or to scare me. I was 16 at the time and it was during my first astral travel experience, so I may have had some fears about evil entities before learning protection techniques. Since then, I've run into evil spirits, but so far, no demons. Real possessions are extremely rare, and other reasons for suspected possession should be thoroughly check out before calling in an expert.

Some UFO and ghost investigators believe that there is a correlation between the Reptilian beings and demons and that they may be one and the same thing. There is much evidence that this is the case. The Reptilian creatures behave and look (scaly skin, vertical pupils, long fingers with claws) as we would expect a demon to—and may indeed be the source of the early Christian ideas about the devil and his minions. I suggest reading David Icke's book *The Biggest Secret*, available at www.davidickebooks.co.uk for more information on this topic.

During trance sessions I have experienced the presence of reptilian-looking creatures who had a negative energy, but did not do any harm to anyone present while we were at the scene of the investigation.

Some people are afraid to contact loved ones because they think the spirit could be a demon masquerading itself. However, if you protect yourself before contacting a spirit and ask to speak only to the person you request, no bad entity can come through. (See how to protect yourself later in this book) I believe that what you experience has to a large extent to do with what you believe. If you believe there are demons out there waiting to get you, they will. If you don't believe that, they probably won't bother you. I do caution you against ghost hunting if any doubts or fears along these lines or you could have a negative experience.

If you feel that a site is truly evil or that there is a demonic possession of the house or people living in it, get help from an expert demonologist like John Zaffis– www.johnZaffis.com, or NEAR-www.nearparanormal.com.

Orbs

Orbs, also known as balls, lights, or globes, are fairly common and many people see them with the naked eye or in photos. Orbs often show up in photographs but can usually be attributed to reflections off of dust, moisture on lenses, lens flare, or an out-of-focus lens. The orbs worth mentioning are the ones that appear to the naked eye and/or and float through space, go through walls or objects, appear to move under intelligent control, and look three-dimensional. If an orb has a face or other shape in it that is also worth noting. Some are very large and others are very tiny.

I've done scans on several orbs in person and in looking at photographs, and have come up with some possibilities as to what they are. In some instances the orb is a spirit. My deceased mother told me that spirits are made up of *light photons*, therefore, wouldn't it stand to reason that the spirit travels as a ball of light? It seems that they do travel from place to place, and time to time for that matter, in this manner then upon arrival may change into a more familiar body so people will recognize them.

Some orbs seem to be spirits that have never lived in a human body. They move about at will, and often appear to be investigating a location before moving on. In some instances orbs have been associated with fairies, sprites, angels, UFO sightings and crop circles, and have been seen moving into a UFO. They may be spirits of aliens, or perhaps are a probe of some sort. In any case, its always exciting to get orbs on film. If you can take video of them you can sometimes tell if it looks like an intelligence is in control as they move about.

Plasma

Plasma is a visible light that appears during lightning storms, can be created by scientists in the lab, and has been seen during crop circle formation and poltergeist activity. It is extremely impressive to watch. Plasma is the fourth state of matter. A plasma is an ionized gas into which sufficient energy is provided to free electrons from atoms or molecules and to allow both ions and electrons, to coexist. It has appeared as very beams or balls of light.

Crop circle researcher Nancy Talbott, the Field Research Coordinator for the *BLT Research Team*, told me that she witnessed a beam of plasma coming from an unknown source outside her window during a visit to The Netherlands. The next morning, there was a gigantic crop circle in the neighboring field. The plasma appeared, as if on cue, right after she expressed the desire to a colleague to see a crop circle being formed. Ms. Talbott surmises that some form of consciousness heard her thoughts and created the circle for her to see. She has photos of this on her website at www.bltresearch.com.

Ball Lightning

I had the opportunity to see ball lighting (or plasma) when I was 10 years of age. There was a lightning storm going on and my father and mother yelled for me to come into the kitchen around 10:00 pm. I was astonished to see a brilliant white ball of light hovering above the open door of the cooking stove. It stayed for a

The above photo was taken by a friend of mine just before her daughter vacated her house due to paranormal activity. I sensed three angry ghosts there, and the foggy orbs may be their spirits.

minute, then disappeared. My father told me it was rare ball lightening that had come down the stove vent, however, I found out later that ball lighting does not appear for more than a couple of seconds. So I am inclined to believe it was something else—maybe plasma or an unknown substance or entity.

Spirit Fog or Vortex

My friend Dennis Kindle gave me the photograph on the previous page, which shows a thick line of white fog that appeared during a spiritual ceremony in the woods in Arkansas right after a three-day crystal dig nearby. The men at the ceremony did not see this at the time, but it showed up on the photo. The ceremony involved creating communication to the spirit world.

What is compelling is that this same zigzag shape is found painted on ancient spiritual sites and caves with petroglyphs, and is believed to be a symbol of communication with spirits.

Spirit Fog during a ceremony
Photo courtesy of Dennis Kindle

The fog is approximately 14" in diameter and goes from the ground up and out of the photo. Note that there are several distinct zigzag formations inside the center of the tube of fog.

There was definitely communication going on at the time the picture was taken. It would be interesting to get some pictures during other spiritual ceremonies to see what shows up. Also note the orb to the left of the fog.

Fog and Apparitions

Fog is less common than the appearance of orbs, but does appear on film and/or to the naked eye. It is often a non-distinct shape, forming and then disappearing, but sometimes forms a human or animal shape that may be very distinct and visible to the naked eye. The most common apparition is formed of a white, almost glowing misty substance. A full apparition, is the appearance of the entire body of a person and a partial apparition, is only part of the person. Some common partial apparitions appear as only the head, or the body without feet.

Some ghost researchers, myself included, think that this is a form that a spirit can take on if they have obtained enough energy to do so. As an example, during a ghost hunt with eleven people, all of the batteries in the camcorders drained at the exact same moment, leaving the batteries in the still cameras alone. A second after that happened, we all saw a foggy apparition appear, although, not fully materialized. My theory is that the ghost needed electrical energy from the batteries in order to form a semi-physical form.

Tree Sprites and Tree Spirits

I have been observing tiny white lights interacting with trees at many locations, but especially in my own backyard. I can only see the lights if I relax my eyes and "see", which is another term for using psychic vision with your eyes. The lights are only visible at night - probably because they would be difficult to see in sunlight. I began concentrating on looking at the lights around one particular

Artistic rendering of tree sprites

tree, and one evening in 2005 I received a telepathic communication to ask the lights what they were. I thought that was strange, but did it nonetheless. To my astonishment, a male voice I've never heard spoke to me telepathically in a clear, loud voice, and said that the lights are the spirits of the tree or "tree sprites."

The sprites informed me that their purpose is to help the tree grow, tell it when to leaf and bud out, when to grow new limbs, and when to go dormant for the winter. One winter I noticed that that the sprites were unusually active, and watched as they made new limbs out of energy, which looked like dark three limbs with a white glow around them.

In the spring I watched carefully to see if new limbs appeared where this energy had been created and sure enough, there were several!

I found out through our "talks" that these spirits have never been in human form, and that their purpose is to assist trees. They stay with the same tree for life, but when the tree dies the sprites will go to another nearby seedling. I've seen these white lights around trees since. Coincidentally, I recently purchased a book called *Irish Tree Spirits*, and after reading through it, I found out that a description I heard during the trance —'Fir Non Goln'—means "Spirits of the Trees."

The tree spirits also let me know that there is a Matrix of energy connecting one tree to the other, so they are connected to every tree on the planet. You can see this energy matrix coming off of each tree, reaching out to nearby trees. This energy looks like a dark line with a white field around it. It is possible to telepathically communicate with a tree, who in turn can request information from fellow trees in other locations and in other times, either in the past, present, or future. This is one way to connect with the Akashic record and get information about anything, including why ghosts haunt a certain location or what happened in the past that would cause a haunting. So trees can be a third-party communicator between an investigator and ghosts.

Aliens

There is quite possibly more evidence that aliens exist than there is evidence about ghosts! Since I have some experience investigating both, there are some similarities between them that you should be aware of.

While ghost hunting you may run into other unexpected entities. There seems to be a correlation between alien and UFO sightings and paranormal activity in many cases.

Vector art
© Albert Ziganshin - Fotolia.com

For instance, several research projects I'm working on that involve abductees or contactees, also involve what seems to be paranormal activity like unexplained sounds, voices, and objects moving, banging noises, missing objects, and orb, fog, and ghost sightings.

Aliens, like ghosts, seem to have the ability to walk through solid walls, appear and disappear at will, and fade in and out. They may be miss-identified as ghosts at times. We don't know yet what the connection is or why so many UFO-related cases also involve paranormal activity, however, there seems to be a pattern that can't be ignored, which is that intuitive or people with psychic abilities seem to experienced both alien and "paranormal' events. Some researchers put all of the above into the "Paranormal" category.

objects, appear and disappear at will, and look transparent or solid. Aliens and ghosts have been caught on film and on voice recorders.

Some people who have had UFO sightings or close encounters also have a "haunted" house. During my investigation of a strange case near Butler, Missouri, we have determined that the connection between aliens and ghosts is probable. The witnesses have obtained multiple photos of not only aliens and craft, but also have seen ghostly apparitions and misty forms taking shape in the same area. Some of these encounters have been in or near graveyards, and others near farms and buildings. The witnesses often have paranormal experiences such as loud banging in the house after going out in the evening to get photographic evidence.

In an effort to get some answers about this strange connection

I asked my mother about it one day, and she not only answered but showed me a scene from the Fifth dimension. In this scene I could see my deceased family members standing in an area along with other ghosts. They seemed to be in groups, floating along in the air above the Earth. Also in the scene were craft and alien beings moving or floating through the area not far from the spirits and live persons travelling in astral bodies.

While I watched this, my mother told me that she and other spirits inhabit the fifth dimension, and that the aliens are from higher dimensions. The aliens and must move through the fifth dimension to get to the third/fourth dimension (Earth). The spirits and aliens did not interact with each other at the time I was watching. My mother told me that she does not communicate with them, but that my grandfather does.

If you want more information about UFOs I suggest reading *Flying Saucers and Science* by nuclear physicist Stanton Friedman, MSc., or *Science Was Wrong* by Stanton Friedman and Kathleen Marden.

Shadow People

Shadow people do not appear to be "people" at all. They are usually described as being very dark, usually darker than a darkened room, or "blacker than night," without defined features, and with or without red glowing eyes. The shadow people with red eyes seem to be more aggressive and want to cause fear. Some have been seen with mitten-line "hands" and others wear a wide-brimmed hat and long frock coat or cloak. The entire entity is black, even the face and hands, and the silhouette is usually of a man. Some have referred to these beings as The Hat People, or the Hat Man, but that may be a different being altogether.

Most encounters are fleeting, such as seeing a shadow out of the corner of the eye, but some reported experiences with shadow people are more frightening.

Drawing by Margie Kay

Some people have awakened in the middle of the night to a crushing feeling on their chest, and see a shadow person kneeling on them, and leaning over them face-to-face in an extremely menacing manner. Many say that they feel that the entity is stealing energy from them, or in some cases they believe that the being is attempting to take their soul or even their life.

My family has had several encounters with shadow people. My oldest daughter saw a dark black entity, blacker than the night, standing in her bedroom when she was thirteen years old. It stood there for at least thirty minutes, not moving, just staring at her. She felt a cold chill in the room and a negative energy, and was very frightened.

My own encounter occurred while driving home one evening after work. I saw a man standing on the steps of a church. He was black from head to toe, and was wearing a long old fashioned late 1800s style frock coat and a wide-brimmed hat. He stood there, staring at a building across the street. I got an eerie feeling and sense of anger from this being. After I passed by I looked in the mirror and he was gone.

My granddaughter awoke one night at 3:00 a.m. to see a shadow man with "mitten" hands standing in her room watching the TV that she had turned off before she went to bed. Only static was on the TV. He was in front and to the side of her, but when she moved he almost immediately turned around to look at her, then disappeared. Since then, she and her family have had numerous sightings of shadow-like shapes and shadow people in their house.

Sightings of shadow people are sometimes the cause of fear and nightmares in children and adults. Perhaps they are the real boogie man in the closet or under the bed. Most paranormal researchers, myself included, do not believe that shadow people are ghosts or disembodied spirits, but are another type of as yet unknown entity. Perhaps they are even from another dimension. The evidence suggests that these beings are a very powerful negative energy that should not be provoked.

I strongly suggest setting up protection around any house where shadow people are seen. (See how to protect yourself later in this book).

Your job as an investigator, is to attempt to determine what or who is doing the haunting, so while ghost hunting keep in mind that everything that happens and everything you see or hear may not be related to a deceased person.

There are also reasons why spirits linger in a certain space—sometimes we cannot understand why they choose to stay here, but there may be a reason why they are just not ready to move on yet. As long as the spirit understands fully that their physical body has died, then I feel it is their choice whether or not they move on now or wait until they are ready. In some cases, the spirit feels that they have unresolved issues that they want to communicate to their loved ones.

I worked on a case for a family who was distraught over the sudden death of their mother and apparent haunting of the house. They could not find a copy of her will. I helped them find it by talking to their mother—it was in a hidden safe in the house. I even got the combination of the safe from their mother. After they had the will in their hands all of the haunting activity stopped. Obviously, this was a case of unresolved issues.

The experiences I have had with ghosts has shown me that life does not end with death of the body. All of us live on in spirit, and in fact, the spirit body is what feels more like "home" to a person than the physical body. My guides tell me that the spirit body is made up of light photons, therefore, I suspect that this may be what the orbs are that we and other ghost hunters catch on film.

My guides also say that we may have thousands of lifetimes on earth or on other planets or dimensions, and that it is even possible to experience several "lives" at the same time. I have known since childhood that the spirit reincarnates and that souls tend to stay with the same family groups. This may be why we often feel as if we have had an experience that we couldn't possibly have had in this lifetime, or sometimes feel out of sorts like we don't "belong" here. If you spent most of your lifetimes on another planet, then decided to see what it was like on Earth, it is easy to see that you might not feel at home for quite some time.

I've found that people who are unable to communicate with spirits are often actually afraid to do so. Their fear of the unknown may be what stops them. I think this fear is largely due to influence from movies, other family members, and maybe their church. People's imagination sometimes gets the better of them, and they may believe that all sorts of bad things will happen if someone communicates with a loved one or spirit who has passed on. In most cases, you will not encounter anything negative, however.

If you can be open to spirits of those who have passed to the other side you may find that they will give you assistance and comfort. Even if you are not able to communicate to the extent that I do, don't be discouraged. Try listening a little closer to that intuition which may warn you of a dangerous situation or help you out with a problem. That intuition may just be your guardian angel, who could be your relative. You've heard the old adage, "Practice makes perfect". The more you acknowledge their presence, the more they will help you.

CHAPTER 4

How to Communicate with Ghosts

I am often asked how a person can learn to see or communicate with ghosts. If you see a ghost, it probably means two things: that your third eye (psychic center located in the center of your forehead) is open, and also that the spirit probably wants you to see him/her.

Spirits inhabit a higher dimension, and it is my opinion that they either have to lower their vibratory rate, or you have to raise your vibratory rate so you can see them, or it may be a combination of both. That is why it is rare to see a clear apparition or catch one on film. Some photographic and infrared equipment capture pictures of ghosts because the equipment is able to "see" a higher level of vibration than humans can (see the chapter on photographing ghosts).

By "vibratory rate" I mean that you must attain or "tune in" to certain levels of frequency in order to view or experience those things that are also on a higher frequency (such as spirits, elementals, or even UFOs). Raising your vibratory rate — and consciousness — may be accomplished in several ways.

My favorite methods are eating a mostly vegetarian diet, spending time in nature and around water, practicing using my psychic abilities, and meditation— which calms the mind and allows you to concentrate on one thing at a time. I highly suggest taking a course or two on meditation if you don't already know how, but following are some tips on how to get started:

Margie's Meditation Method

Meditation can help you get to the Beta level of consciousness, where psychic abilities are more easily accessed. At the Beta level our brain waves average at around 12—15 cycles per second. At Theta state brainwaves are between 6-7 HZ , and at Alpha (normal waking and relaxed state) brainwaves are between 7 and 12 HZ. Beta level is the state we try to achieve before contacting the other side.

1.) Pick a time to practice every day, preferably at night when it is quiet and there is little activity going on. Try to stick to the same time every day. I meditate just before going to bed.

2.) Pick a place to meditate that is comfortable and where you won't be disturbed by people, pets, or loud noises like traffic or trains.

3.) Either sit in an easy chair, or lie down on a bed or couch and use pillows or blankets to get very comfortable. I prefer to lie down because it is more comfortable for me. If you fall asleep while meditating don't worry about it. *Note: Meditation before sleep often allows you to have a deeper, more restful sleep.*

4.) Use of a meditation CD is a good way to get the brain down to beta state fairly quickly. Listen to the music and relax. If you don't have a CD, just listen to your own breathing for a few

minutes. I can highly recommend Janalea Hoffman's CDs (see the resource listing)
to help you get to a very relaxed state.

5.) Get relaxed: start at your toes and flex, then relax your muscles from your feet to the top of your head. Start with the feet muscles, then calves, then thighs, etc. all the way to your neck and head. Go back a couple of times to the jaw and neck areas, since this is the area where people hold the most tension. Take your time and don't rush the process. After using this method for a few months, you'll get very adept at relaxing and won't have to go through the entire process anymore. Your entire body will relax at your suggestion.

6.) Clear your mind. You can do any number of activities at this point, based on what your goals are. If you want to contact a loved one who has passed on, or a spirit who is haunting a house, ask to be in contact with that person. Visualize them standing in front of you. When you have a clear picture, ask the person a question and listen for a response. If you don't succeed at first, keep trying. After several sessions you should be able to hear or "feel" the answer. Be sure to write down everything that happened after you stop meditating.

Another project you may want to do while meditating is to create something. First visualize a blank black curtain in front of you. Then visualize whatever it is you would like to manifest in your life—a loved one who passed on that you would like to communicate with, or money, love, a house, job, travel, health, or whatever you wish. Concentrate on that and say to yourself "This manifests for me now" or something similar, over and over again until you feel confident that you have created this in your life. Believe that this is happening, and it will happen.

Always use positive words instead of negative words. For instance, say "I am completely healthy" instead of "I don't have arthritis," since the subconscious mind understands only what you are concentrating on.

Start with small things that are easier to obtain before moving on to bigger, more important things. You'll be surprised how your life can change using meditation on a daily basis. Don't be discouraged if you have trouble relaxing and concentrating at first. A lot of people find it very difficult to stop for 15-30 minutes a day after a hectic day.

Your mind has to get used to the change, and it may take a while— but after a few weeks you'll start to feel more confident and it will get easier and easier.

A way to get to "level" faster is to use a meditation CD such as Immrama Insight (www.immramainstitute.org) or one of Janalea Hoffman's CDs (www.rhythmicmedicine.com).

I have been meditating for over thirty years, and I strongly believe that it has helped me train my mind to the point that I can instantly go into a trance to do work on investigations or ghost hunting. You will get to the stage where you can have dual-consciousness, which means that part of your mind is in a trance state, and part of your mind is fully awake, alert, and communicating with others around you.

Other ways to raise your level of consciousness and vibratory rate:

•**Eat a vegetarian, or mostly vegetarian diet.** The lighter foods will bring your frequency up. It may take a while to take effect if you are a meat eater and your body will go through withdrawals for a while. After a few weeks you won't miss meat at all.

•**Drink very little alcohol.** Alcohol lowers your frequency to very low levels—and actually makes you very vulnerable to attack by mischievous entities. Drink no more than a glass of wine or beer a day. I only have one or two per month.

•**Don't have too much sugar**– many people experience a literal "buzz" when they have sugar. It really upsets the balance of your system and is quite harmful physically as well as psychically. Also do not use artificial sweeteners—I believe that they have a disruptive vibration.

•**Don't smoke.** You know the physical reasons, but it also dramatically inhibits psychic awareness.

•**Practice dowsing.** Dowsing puts you in contact with your higher self through the lower self, or subconscious, who will assist you with all spiritual matters, including awareness. Check out some books on dowsing or take a dowsing class to get started. See the section on dowsing later in this book.

•**Stop hanging around negative people.** If there are any negative people in your life, consider stopping the relationship. Other than the psychological reasons for staying in a positive environment, negative energies from others bring your own energy levels down.

•**Practice "*seeing*."** There is a certain technique to use in order to see auras, energy, and sometimes ghosts. It is called "*seeing*." The method is to relax the eyes rather than staring hard, and is the opposite of what most people think must be used. By relaxing the eyes, you will be using the rods in the eyes, which are photoreceptor cells used for dim-light vision, rather than the cones, which are responsible for daytime and color vision. If you haven't tried this before, you will be in for a treat. You will see things that you never imagined, most likely starting with electromagnetic energy fields around living things. This method alone may be enough for you to see spirits.

•**Practice telepathy games with other people.** Practice makes perfect with anything, so why not psychic abilities? If you use it all the time you'll get good at it. The QUEST Investigation Group routinely practices using several methods in order to keep sharp and learn new skills. Some of the things we practice are listed on the next page.

1. The missing person: Have someone go outside and stand somewhere on your property while you stay inside in a location where you can't see out windows or doors. Have the person notify you by walkie-talkie or cell phone that they are in position. Tell them to visualize where they are. Now close your eyes and try to pick up the message from that person—look around and see if you can tell where the location is. At first you may only get colors or shapes. After a while, you may get pretty good at it. This can also be done with objects that you can have someone hide inside or outside the house.

2. Playing cards: Using a set of standard playing cards, have someone else pick out cards and look at them, one at a time, while you write down which card you think it is. To make it easier to start with, just take 5 or 6 cards from the deck to use at one time. Work up to using the entire deck. Try to relax while you are doing this and you'll have better results. Write down the first thing that comes to your mind, and don't "overthink" it. Your first impulse is usually the right one.

3. The number game: Have one or more people write down and concentrate on a number between 1 and 10. Write down what you think it is. Do this at least 20 times per session. Taking turns with other people makes it more fun.

4. Use Zener Cards: This is a set of 25 cards used in testing for ESP designed by Karl Zener, a Swiss Psychologist and his associate J.B. Rhine, at Duke University in the 1930s. The cards are designed to test psychic abilities. Each set contains five of each of the following cards: Circle, Square, Three wavy lines, Five-pointed star, and Circle. To use, have someone shuffle the deck and look at a card, while you try to perceive what it is. Keep a record of your tests. It is best if you have a third party write down the findings so the results are accurate and unbiased. A result of 25% or more in accuracy indicates psychic ability.

You can make up other games and tests on your own and use the ones you like the best. It is a good idea to keep a notebook with records of all of your practice sessions so you can see your progress. You'll probably find that your skills will improve over time. The more you practice, the faster the results.

Hypnosis

Hypnosis is a method used to access the subconscious mind and communicate with it. The use of hypnosis can access a deeper level of mind than normal mediation can, and in some cases, the person can go deep enough that the hypnotist is able to communicate with other beings outside the self. This can be useful if trying solve a difficult case, but hardly practical for frequent use.

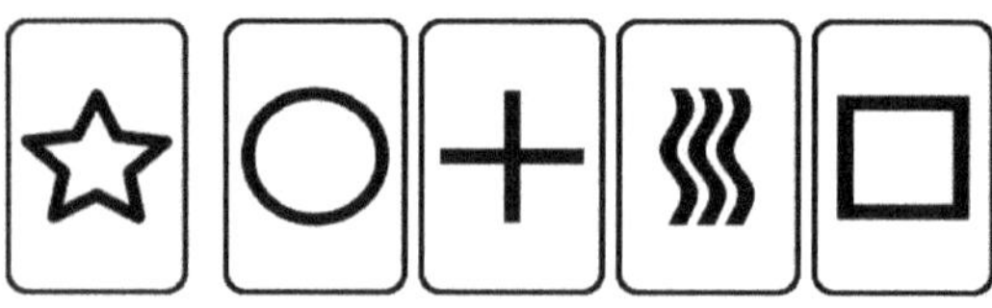

The Zener Cards

It might be worthwhile to have several sessions with a certified hypnotist to help you relax and learn how to get in touch with your subconscious mind. For most people, they find it easier to meditate on their own after several hypnosis sessions with a professional. See the Resources section for my recommended hypnotist source.

Sometimes *seeing* ghosts is just a matter of *wanting* to see them. I believe that most places are haunted and there are spirits around us all the time since I see them often, so it is just a matter of finding out what the best technique is for you to be able to communicate with them.

Don't be discouraged if you just can't see anything, however. If you sense there is a presence nearby, use your pendulum and ask questions that way. (See my dowsing techniques later in this book)

How to Communicate with Ghosts Using Your Sixth Sense

After you've practiced some of the techniques mentioned previously, it is time to practice seeing, hearing, or feeling spirits. Using the sixth sense—clairvoyance, clairaudience, and clairsentience—means being able to trust observations that are much more subtle than everyday experiences. The world of the psychic is much different. It is difficult to explain, but once you experience it, you'll know what it is.

Clairsentience is the first intuitive talent that people report having. It means that you sense something without benefit of seeing or hearing it. You just "know" something. This is the first stage of psychic awareness, and is usually called "intuition" by lay-persons. Intuition is associated with persons who know that aunt Betty is going to call on the phone in a few minutes, or that someone is talking about them at that moment. But it can go beyond that to include investigative work such as ghost hunting, and can be used to sense what happened at a location and who is doing the haunting.

The intuitive learns to trust what he sees or hears or feels that is beyond the normal five senses. This is difficult at first, because it may not seem "real." The reality is, however, that intuition *is* real, and it becomes more clear as you practice using these talents. For instance, if you stick your hand in a freezer, you will instantly feel physically cold, but if a spirit passes by you may feel a coldness, or sense a coldness, which in most cases will be much less obvious than the freezer cold. This is one example of the subtleness of the experience.

Clairvoyance is the ability to use your third eye, rather than your physical eyes. Some people call this technique Remote Viewing. I close my eyes when contacting spirits because I see better that way using my third eye. When I want to see a physical manifestation however, I'll switch to using my physical eyes in the relaxed state mentioned earlier.

When looking with your physical eyes you may see apparitions, fog, mist, orbs, shadows, or shapes. On some investigations I've seen strange shapes appear such as a music stand, a cane, an umbrella, and a ball. All of these things were significant to a particular investigation, and all of them appeared as black shapes, not in color.

Using the third eye is quite different. What you need to see or what is important will appear to you very clearly, in color, with enough light to get a good picture. For me it is like watching a movie. If I want to go back in time to watch a particular event, I'll often see the location with all of the surroundings, the people present, what they were wearing, etc. However, this method is not 100% accurate when it comes to timing of the event. Time is the absolute hardest thing to get, and any clairvoyant will tell you the same thing. If you ask to go to a particular date, you'll have more luck than if you ask what the date was of an event. This must have something to do with our perception of time. In order to get around this problem, I'll often look around the room I'm visiting for a newspaper or magazine with a date on it and sometimes I'll get lucky.

When in "third eye" mode, the people or spirits I talk with appear alone, usually with no surroundings or distractions. They look very clear to me, but every little detail may not always be apparent unless they want me to see something of importance. It might be important to be able to identify the spirit, so they often show me a tattoo or scar in order for me to be sure I'm talking to the right person.

In order to get to the state of consciousness necessary to use the third eye, I go into what I call a "dual state of consciousness." For me, this means that part of me is fully conscious, and part of me is in a trance-like state. I believe that my years of meditation practice and practice using my psychic abilities every day allows me to do that. For others it may also be very easy to learn how to do, but for some not so easy. I suggest practicing getting to this state of mind in order to become more proficient. Hypnosis sessions seem to speed this along. If you've ever been hypnotized, you may remember the feeling of part of you sinking and letting go, yet having a part of you observe the process at the same time. That observer part is the conscious state.

I simply ask to go to a particular time and place where an event happened that may be important to the case. If possible, I sit in a comfortable recliner, but if not, I can do this standing if it is just for a short time. I have someone with me at all times to record when I'm doing trance work because sometimes I forget what I saw or said, or in come cases, did. This may be a sign of getting older, but I suggest having someone with you or use a recorder in order to have an accurate record of events. When I investigated a suicide in 1985, my hand went into the shape of a gun and I raised it to my temple without knowing it, and the observers around me saw that happen. While I did not "see" what the method of death was at the time, the person had indeed shot himself in the temple.

It is important to be very observant while doing trance work because solving the puzzle may be in the details. Look around at buildings, inside rooms, at paperwork, books, desks, and of course, people. Observe what the people are wearing, how they interact with each other, their facial expressions, and what they do.

Sometimes you'll be drawn to look at something that your analytical mind wants to ignore, but don't give into that feeling. Go ahead and take a look at whatever it is that you are drawn to because it may be very significant. One case in particular comes to mind, when I was drawn to look at food on the table, then rat poison in the kitchen cabinet. Careful observation of the death of the person indicated that he had indeed been poisoned but that no one knew about it. His spirit lingered because he wanted justice, even though all of the people involved had been long gone. I worked with him and was able to get him to move on.

Clairaudience is simply hearing the other side. Usually, this means hearing the voice of a spirit talking, but can also be the sounds of a plane, traffic, or other things that might be an important part of a message. If a person is trying to communicate that he was killed by a train I may hear a train whistle blowing, or if they were murdered by gun I'll hear the gunshot.

The ability to hear the other side comes in very handy when dealing with the spirit world because the spirits can tell you exactly what happened and why they haunt. I've heard it all —and here are some samples of what the spirits have said:

"I was wronged and I want revenge"
"This is my favorite place and I just like to visit."
"This is my house and everyone needs to get out!"
"This is where I died, and this is where I'll stay."
"I'm looking for my mommy."
"Where is my family?"
"Why can't my family see or hear me?"
"What are you doing in my house?"
" I killed him/her because ___________."
"This is none of your business."

When you take the role of the psychic, remote viewer, or intuitive, you also take on the responsibility for communicating with the dead and helping them understand that they have died and nothing can be done about that. You'll want to make them understand that they need to move on with their spirit guides, family, or angels that are waiting for them. If this is something you want to do but are still having trouble with after using the techniques outlined in this book, I suggest taking some classes at your local metaphysical book store, Transcendental Meditation Center, or check online for classes at other locations near you. Large conferences also often have workshops on hypnosis, remote viewing, psychic training, and more. I can recommend Deloris Cannon's hypnosis workshops and certified hypnotists – visit www.ozarkmt.com for more information.

Many people wonder why spirits don't give us the lottery numbers or give us exact dates of future events, or warn us about catastrophes. The fact is, that no one has the answers to those questions. Occasionally, you'll hear about someone winning the Powerball who says they got the numbers from their deceased grandfather in a dream. And my own grandfather seems to specialize in showing me pictures of future world events, and has been correct about the next volcano, earthquakes, and tsunami's many times. However, getting an exact date about an event seems to be the most difficult, probably since the spirit world, or fifth dimension, does not experience time as we know it.

When researching past events, however, the spirits seem to be very willing and helpful, often giving precise information like dates, names, and addresses. That makes communication with ghosts through telepathy a useful tool to use when ghost hunting.

The world of ghost hunting is what some call paranormal, and that, in my opinion, is because we just don't fully understand what 'normal' is yet. That is to say, the spirit world is most likely a natural, normal event and place, and that just because science doesn't fully understand it yet, is not proof that it doesn't exist.

Those of us who hunt ghosts do so mostly because we are looking for enough evidence to convince ourselves and the skeptics that there is life after death of the body. If you are new to ghost hunting, please try some of the scientific and intuitive techniques listed in this book and I can almost guarantee success in contacting spirits from the other side.

Are You Psychic?

Take this test to see if you can see ghosts now, without any training or practice:

1.) Do you ever have the feeling of being watched when no one is around?

2.) Have you ever had a dream that later came true?

3.) Do you dream in color and in great detail?

4.) Have you ever had a Déjà vu experience?

5.) Did you ever know that someone was going to call you, then the phone rang and it was them?

6.) Are you open-minded about the paranormal?

7.) Do you meditate on a regular basis?

8.) Have you ever had a strong feeling about something, such as not to drive on a certain street, only to find out later that there was a reason?

9.) Do you wear black most of the time?

10.) Does psychic ability run in your family?

11.) Are you more creative/artistic than logical/analytical?

12.) Do you have success when dowsing or using a spirit board or similar device?

If you answered yes to seven or more questions above, you already have some psychic ability, and just need to work on some of the techniques mentioned in this book to expand your mind. A "yes" answer to all of the above means that you are extremely psychic and are probably already seeing ghosts. If you answered yes to less than seven questions, keep working and your skills will improve as long as you have an open mind.

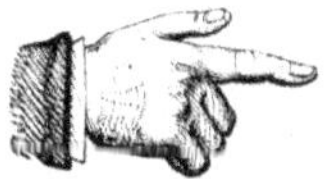

TIP:

Don't be discouraged if you can't see ghosts—It doesn't mean they aren't there, and it doesn't mean that you can't get evidence by other means.

CHAPTER 5

Ghost Hunting Tools and Techniques

It is good practice to use scientific means to obtain evidence of ghosts, however, keep in mind that it may take hours, days, or weeks before getting evidence of a haunting using these methods. The ideal investigation would include setting up cameras and voice recorders for a day or a week prior to doing an on-site investigation, in order to get as much evidence as possible, but that is not practical for most weekend ghost hunters. Most of us have full-time jobs and don't have the resources or time needed to do scientific investigations, nevertheless, hobby ghost hunters have gotten some good video, voice, and photographic evidence, not to mention the tactile evidence experienced on the scene.

Following is a list of items and their functions, which can be useful in confirming an anomalous presence. Practicing ghost hunters usually keep their equipment in a "Ghost Hunting Bag", which is always ready to go.

Laser Thermometer: This is a high-tech gadget that my husband uses for his outdoor brick bake oven, and I use in the field when ghost hunting. You just aim it at a surface and pull the trigger to see what the temperature is. Often we will find a drop or rise in temperature in a location where we see or sense a spirit. It is a good device to use to prove that there is something anomalous about an area.

Digital Thermometer: Since a laser thermometer is limited to detecting surface temperature, I also carry a digital thermometer which reads the ambient room temperature. This can be quite useful when a drop in temperature is noted in specific spots in mid-air. An extremely cold spot can be indicative that a spirit is present.

EMF Detector: This handy gadget detects electromagnetic fields around any electronic device but may also "spike" when a spirit is nearby. Be careful to check for any electrical wires or junction boxes, computers, radios, or TVs in the area that may cause high readings. In the absence of any electronics or wiring, you can be reasonably sure that there is another cause for any high readings.

Digital Cameras and Video: We have four digital cameras and one professional Sony HI-8 camcorder, as well as "trip cameras" which get set up in rooms where a lot of activity is suspected. Movement triggers the camera to take a picture and it is totally silent. Just leave it alone after setting up and check the memory card later, and you may be surprised at what the camera picks up.

We have used digital cameras and digital video cameras to get images of orbs, foggy shapes, shadows, and occasionally a spirit. Sometimes things show up on disk that can't by seen with the naked eye. We never manipulate photos except to lighten or darken and add contrast if needed to see objects better.

In an emergency situation you may be able to use a cell phone camera.

Be sure to take along extra charged batteries since it is common for ghosts to drain power sources. I keep my spare batteries in the car, away from the investigation site just in case a ghost drains all of the batteries at the same location at the same time. It is thought that spirits need energy to materialize and take it from the nearest source, which may be your camera batteries.

Motion-Activated Digital Camera: Available online, these inexpensive cameras (also known as hunter cameras) can be mounted on a wall and take a picture automatically when there is any movement in the area, and with little or no noise. A memory card in the camera can be removed and reviewed later for evidence, and the larger the card, the more photos can be stored. I suggest placing one or more of these cameras in highly active rooms at different heights. You may leave the room in order to investigate other areas. Make sure there are no house pets around that may trip the camera. Both indoor and outdoor motion-activated cameras are available.

Night Vision Monocular or Binoculars: This is a single-or double eye piece device that allows a person to see in pitch darkness or with very little light. We sometimes pick up spirits with it, then try to take a photo of the same area. Check out hunting gear suppliers for good night vision monocular. I find it difficult to hold and look through this small view finder for more than a few minutes. Toy stores have new night vision head gear for kids that work very well and are easier to use. These only have a 50-foot range, but for ghost hunting you shouldn't need more than that. You may be surprised at what else you can see with this device—UFO hunters are now using longer range night vision gear to see UFOs. Note: never aim the device at a source of light or your retinas could be injured.

Digital Voice Recorder: We use this to capture answers from ghosts. This is commonly known as an EVP (Electronic Voice Phenomena). Someone holds the recorder while asking a question, then pauses to allow time for a spirit to answer. Often when we play back the recorder a ghostly voice will have replied that we didn't hear at the investigation. Sometimes during an investigation I will hear a voice reply to me but others around me don't hear it, then when we play back the recorder others can hear it. Get one that has at least four hours of recording time.

Wind Meter: Used to measure any breeze inside buildings that may indicate a ghostly presence. Be careful to thoroughly check for any other source of air movement due to fans, open windows and doors, etc. before attributing it to a ghost. Sudden breezes from nowhere may be an indication of ghostly activity.

Pendulums and Dowsing Rods: Pendulums and dowsing rods are very handy to use on an investigation because we can often get immediate answers to yes or no questions or help in guiding us where to go on a site. I always carry a pendulum with me just in case I need it. See "How to Dowse" to learn more about dowsing.

UV Light: We have done some experimenting done using UV lights that are used in HVAC equipment to kill bacteria after I got a telepathic communication from my mother from the other side. She suggested that we would be able to see ghosts better that way. Backlights have also proved useful for this purpose.

Psychics: Don't forget to take along someone who is clairvoyant, clairsentient, or clairaudient! This can be invaluable when trying to

Make Your Own Ghost Communicator

An Inexpensive DIY project

1.) Obtain a 6-foot or longer length of 6" - 8" diameter single wall B-vent chimney pipe (available at hardware stores) or single-wall black chimney pipe.

2.) Place the pipe right in front of a fan. You may need to raise the pipe on some books, or place it on a table with the fan on a chair. Be sure to place the fan setting on non-oscillating. The smaller the fan the better, however, higher fan speeds seem to work better. I don't suggest using CPU Fans because they aren't strong enough.

3.) Place a digital recorder near the opposite end of the pipe, ask questions and listen carefully. You may be surprised to hear voices clearly from the other side.

determine why a ghost is haunting a place, what they want, and sometimes you can find out what their name is and the year they died. After getting this information, you may want to go to the local public library or county clerk's office and see if you can find records that match what you find at the site. Some psychics are able to communicate with spirits and ask them to move on (if that is the desire) or get detailed information that is not obtainable any other way.

White Noise: Use of a television turned to a channel with no programming, or a radio tuned to a frequency without programming in order to hear or see ghosts. White noise CDs are also available. It is thought that ghosts are able to communicate more easily while white noise is played. Try using this method while filming or audio recording the session. Ask questions, then allow time for a response. You may hear responses or the responses may be captured on a recording device.

Wind or Fan: One day I tried this technique after a communication with my mother, who suggested it so that others in the family could hear her speak. We used a small oscillating fan during the first session, and my daughter and I clearly heard my mother's voice call my daughter's name. I have used fans and wind, and even whole-house heating and air conditioning vents with successful results when contacting spirits. If it is windy, go outside and ask questions, then listen to the wind. Also try putting a fan on low speed and stand in front of it, or sit next to a vent in a house while the air conditioning or heat is on. Ask questions and listen carefully. We have received some very clear replies using these methods that everyone on the ghost hunting team can hear. I would call this another "White Noise" method, since noise is produced by the fan.

Your Ghost Hunting Kit

All serious ghost hunters need to have a ghost hunting kit that is ready to go at a moment's notice. I use a black duffle bag with outside pockets on it for small things. If you keep everything in one place you'll never be looking for stuff before you go on a hunt. Pack these items in your bag:

- Flashlights with red gel coverings so you can see in the dark but not be blinded (available at Wal-Mart)
- Note pads and pens
- Digital recorders
- Digital camera
- Motion-activated camera(s)
- Video camera
- Night Vision Camera (try I-GEN 20/20)
- EMF detector
- Spare batteries for everything
- Crystals for protection and communication
- Night vision goggles or monocular
- Night vision camera
- Compass
- Walkie-talkies
- Chairs to sit on if doing outside work
- Mosquito repellant
- First aid kit

And don't forget to take your cell phone!

Communication Device: Bring along a round pencil or short dowel rod, tennis ball, marbles, or other objects that can be easily moved. Place the object on a smooth surface and ask the spirit if it can move the object. If it can, ask it to move in answer to your questions. A "yes" answer indicated by a moving object, and a "no" answer is no movement. Be sure to have your video camera aimed at the object. It is often easier for spirits to communicate in this manner.

Drinking Glass: For a group to use to contact spirits. Useful when used on a smooth-surface table that has been painted with "yes," "no," and/or letters for the spirit to communicate with. The method is to have each person place one finger on the bottom of the overturned glass, ask a question, and wait for an answer. A round table works best.

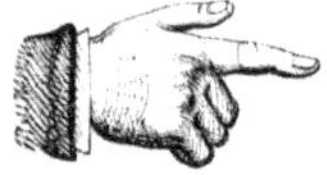

TIP:

The subconscious mind does not understand "good" from "bad," only that it will manifest what you concentrate on or visualize. Therefore, try to keep the thoughts in mind that you want to have happen, rather than focusing on the negative for better results.

CHAPTER 6

How to Dowse for Spirits

Dowsing, also known as "water witching" or "divining" is a practice that has been around for thousands of years. It works well to find water or minerals, and for ghost hunting as well. Many people who have learned how to dowse do it on a daily basis to find missing objects, or even to use as a diagnostic tool. After learning how to dowse, you may want to get in the habit of carrying a pendulum with you at all times - you'll be glad to have it with you to use as a tool when you need it.

Who is Answering When You Dowse?

When dowsing, your are in contact with your Higher self, who knows everything and communicates with you through your subconscious or Lower self. The Lower self uses the muscles and energy in and around your body to make a dowsing tool react and give you answers. It does this my moving a pendulum, L-rods, wood Y-rods, or any other dowsing device. In essence, you are talking to yourself when you dowse. If you clear properly (see description following) you will be sure to communicate only with your Lower and Higher self.

Clear First

Always clear yourself and the area before dowsing in order to remove any negativity or thoughts that could confuse the answers you get from the pendulum. Ask to be in contact with your higher self, then ask your higher self to do a clearing. The pendulum will move in a clockwise direction until it is finished, then will stop.

How to Use a Pendulum

You can use any device that is heavy enough to move when dangled —such as keys, a pendant, or a purchased pendulum made out of stone, crystal, or brass. The higher self seems to be able to communicate easier when using natural materials. I seem to have the best luck with heavier brass pendulums and prefer to use the "UFO" style. I also keep a quartz crystal pendant around my neck that serves double duty for protection and as a pendulum. You might consider wearing a similar type of pendant that can also be used as a pendulum when you need it, or carry a small pendulum in your pocket.

The Pendulum Answers

You can use any directions you like, but the most common method is to ask the pendulum to move in a clockwise direction for a "yes" answer, a counter-clockwise direction to indicate a "no" answer, and straight up and down for a "maybe" or "not quite" answer. You may also want to ask the pendulum to return to this position in-between questions so it is ready to answer quickly.

If desired, you can also ask the pendulum to stop or say "ok" after you get an answer so it will not keep on moving. When first using a pendulum, you should indicate which directions are to mean which answers. In essence, you are telling the pendulum your preferred method of communication.

Asking Questions

It is usually easiest to ask for "yes" or "no" answers to questions, but there are times when you may want to use the pendulum in different ways. If you look on the front of the chart on the next page, there are a set of numbers in a arch shape. If you are looking for a number answer, it is faster to hold the pendulum in the arch area below the numbers and ask it to point in the direction of the number you are looking for. It will start moving in a straight line towards that number. Similarly, you may ask for a yes, no, maybe, or try again later answer by holding the pendulum over the words and waiting for a "yes" clockwise response.

The more you dowse, the better you'll get, and the faster the responses will be to your questions. Try to allot a few minutes a day to dowsing, and you'll have it down in no time. Don't be discouraged if at first you don't get immediate answers—the pendulum needs to warm up to your energies and your subconscious and higher self need to get used to the idea that you wish to contact them on a regular basis.

How to Use Dowsing Rods

Dowsing rods or "L-Rods" are used differently than a pendulum. Most dowsers use rods when looking for something like water or minerals, but they can be used to send you in the direction of anything, including ghosts. Some dowsing rods have witness chambers in them on the ends where you can place an item that is the same thing you are looking for, i.e. gold or silver. For ghost hunting, however, the witness chamber is not practical to use. Dowsing L-Rods have a handle with a hole drilled in it to allow the rod to move freely.

Hold the dowsing rods in your hands and place your thumb over the top of the movable part to stead it until you are ready to start dowsing. Hold the rods at a 90-degree angle to your body. Now think about what you want to find and ask a question such as "If there is a ghost here, where is it?" You should feel a pull on the rods, which will usually move to the right or left, then straighten out when you are headed in the right direction, then pull you towards the ghost or whatever you are looking for. The rods will then cross over each other when you are in the right spot.

The pull of energy can be quite strong at times, especially for experienced dowsers. I believe this has to do with the energy exchange between the dowser and the rods. In order to get an accurate reading, keep your mind focused on the object you are searching for and try to keep distractions to a minimum when you are first learning to do this.

You may want to practice searching for different things for a couple of weeks for car keys or items people can hide for you before using the rods as a ghost hunting tool. I also find the rods useful for finding gravestones or locating where a fellow ghost hunter is on the scene.

Note: Use the Dowsing Assistant on the next page to get answers with a pendulum. Copy and enlarge if desired.

TIP:

In an emergency, use wire hangers instead of metal dowsing rods. Hold one hanger in each hand on the wide bottom side, with the hooks pointing down.

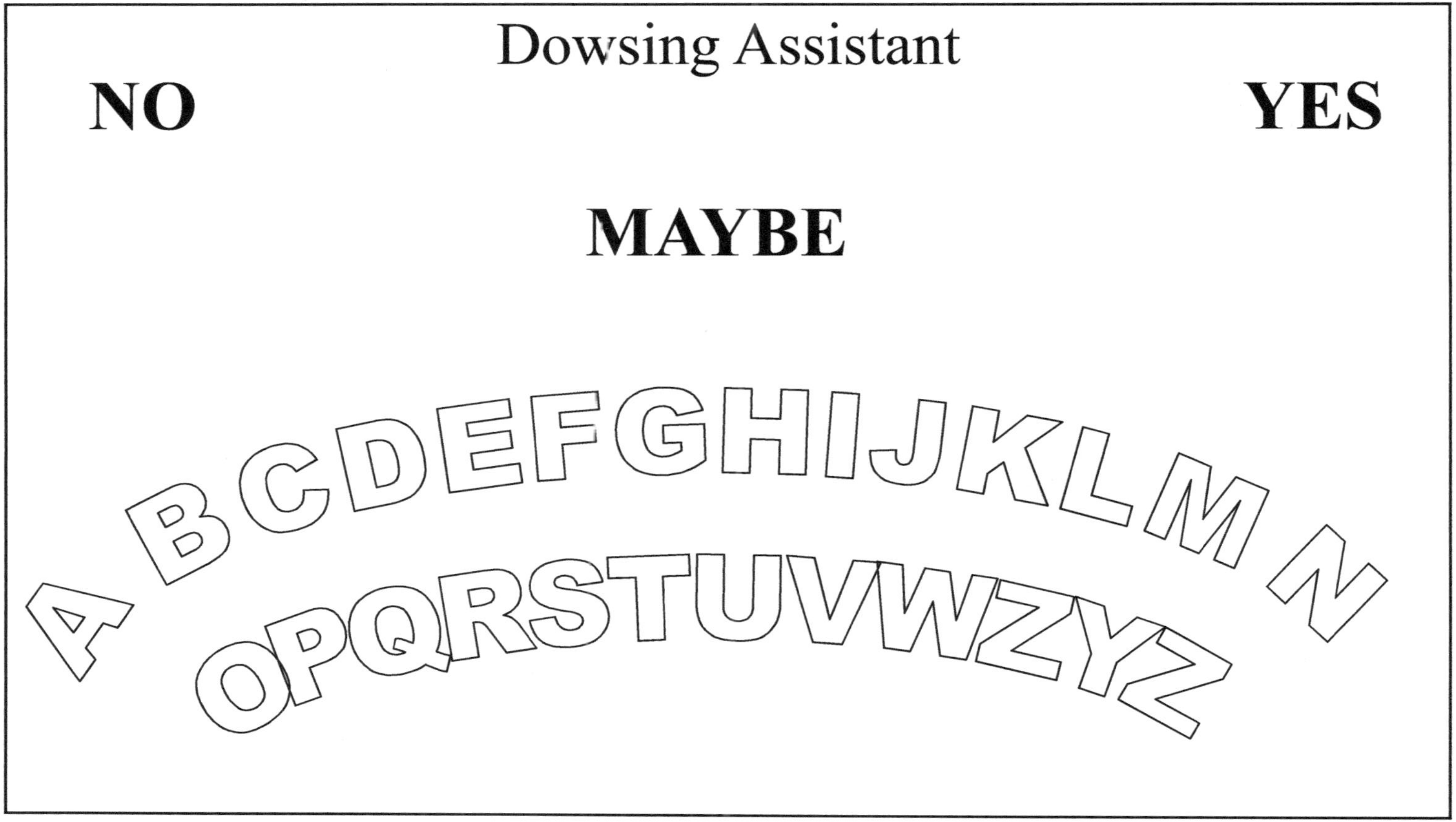

Dowsing Assistant

NO **YES**

MAYBE

A B C D E F G H I J K L M N

O P Q R S T U V W Z Y Z

CHAPTER 7

Photographing Ghosts

This is probably the most frustrating part of ghost hunting. A picture is the evidence that most of us want to get as proof of a spirit's existence. Yet invariably, we don't have a camera available when we see something, or when we don't see anything we don't use the camera.

I encourage you to take photos of nothing. Yes, nothing. Just take pictures of everything around you, even aim the camera behind your head while you are facing forward. You'll be pleasantly surprised at what turns up in photos taken with any type of camera, when you may not have seen anything unusual at the time you took the picture. And if you do sense that there is something in the area, by all means snap some pictures.

Take your still camera or video camera with you everywhere, and when you get the chance, or have a feeling that there may be spirits in the area, snap some pictures. With digital cameras you can easily delete any photos that don't show anything so you don't waste film.

You might want to get out your old photo albums and start thumbing through them to see if there is anything anomalous that you may have missed. Orbs, mist, fog, and apparitions have shown up on some of our 35 mm, old Polaroid cameras and newer digital photographs that we missed before we were actually looking for anything out of the ordinary.

Rotary Park Stream Area
Courtesy of Quest Investigation Group
(Brightness increased to see orbs better)

This is a photo taken of an area where we sensed spirits near a stream. I've seen the ghost of an old prospector from the early to mid 1800s here whenever we visit the park. While in a "Dual Consciousness" state I view the area and see a tent with a fire in front of it, and the man panning gold in the stream and tending his cook pot over the fire. The man does not like people to bother him and he still hangs out at his "claim" many years later. Note several orbs in the picture.

Unidentified light sources Street light

Rotary Park, Independence
Unknown light sources—Quest Investigation Group

This very unusual photo was taken at a park during a ghost hunting expedition. No one saw any of the three lights at the left at the time the photo was taken but after they showed up on the computer, two of us returned to the exact same spot at the same time of night and could find no sources of light that could explain it. The light at the right is a streetlight in the park. Notice the white blurry light coming from the street light just outside the upper left corner of the photo. The light streaks are extremely bright even though this was on a foggy night. When I took this photo I sensed a lot of activity in the area and felt something watching me but did not see anything with the naked eye.

Courtesy of HearthMasters, Inc.

A stream of spirit fog in front of a house. This was not visible to the naked eye at the time the photo was taken.

Courtesy of HearthMasters, Inc.

This photo was taken by a chimney inspector on a clear day. He was just taking a picture of the chimney, but when I printed this out all of these orbs showed up. They are all different colors. Most paranormal investigators I've showed this to agree that the colored orbs are rare. Note the half orbs at the bottom of the photo.

Rotary Park, Independence, Missouri
Courtesy QUEST Investigation Group

The photograph above was taken right after a ghost hunt at a local park. Two of us sensed a presence in the area and took several pictures with digital cameras. Most of the photos showed nothing unusual, but this one has an orb in the picture.

There is no orb in other photos taken before or after these in the same location. So that means that within a few seconds, something anomalous showed up. It is a good idea to take lots of pictures of the same location for this reason. See the full investigation story later in this book.

A possible angel in the clouds?
Photographed by my sister-in-law in 2005.

"Annie Tree" in Independence, Missouri
Photo Courtesy QUEST Investigation Group

I believe that this tree is inhabited by Annie Ralston-James (Frank James' wife) at Rotary Park in Independence, MO. *Note the orb in the upper left corner of the photo.* Frank James was the brother of the famous outlaw Jesse James. The brothers lived in the Independence area for while. Annie first told me her name during a visit to the park in 2003, and she is always in this tree when I visit the area. One spot in front of the tree is always several degrees warmer than anywhere around it, and this has been measured with a laser thermometer.

Annie's apparition has appeared on numerous occasions to many witnesses. She wears a long old-fashioned dress. Annie was a schoolteacher in a school very near this spot. She and her husband, Frank James are buried at the top of Hill Park across 23rd street.

Photo courtesy of Kent Dicus

Another example of anomalies in photographs that were not visible at the time the photo was taken is this photo with Kent Dicus of Kansas City standing by the grave of his great-great-aunt, Mary "Mollie" Thomas Dobyns DeHaven at the Walnut Grove Cemetery in Boonville, MO on August 10, 2002.

Kent and his friend, Michael (the photographer) did not see anything out of the ordinary at the time of their visit to the cemetery, However, after developing this photograph they noticed a profile of a person's face behind the grave marker just to the right of Kent.

Neither man has any idea what this clear apparition could be. There is no way a person could stand behind the cross without being seen. Kent and Michael have returned to the same location several times to see if they could find an explanation for this, but have been unable to find anything out of the ordinary.

Also note what appears to be a stream of energy above the column-like marker in the upper right of the picture.

This photo was taken in my sister-in-law's garden (we call it the Fairy Garden) on a clear day with no fog present. The fog was not visible to the eye. This area is where small balls of light have been spotted.

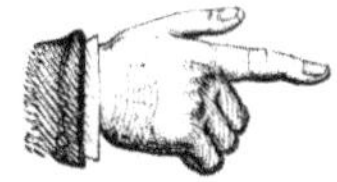

TIP:

Always get permission from landowners or business owners before ghost hunting on their property, and check for closing times in graveyards.

Older homes with a lot of history, like the Vaile Mansion in Independence, Missouri may be haunted.

CHAPTER 8

Good Places to Find Ghosts

There are lots of places that are haunted. Besides the obvious graveyards, old forts, historic buildings, Colonial and Victorian homes, there are many other places to look.

One late afternoon just as a test I "turned on" my third eye while driving just to see how many places harbor ghosts in my neighborhood in Independence, Missouri. I drove around the Independence Square, and down Lexington and Short streets, down Winner Road and then Sterling. I was amazed at how many spirits inhabit the houses— in fact, probably 80% of the homes had a ghostly presence. Most were ghosts of elderly people who had lived in the homes. Some were younger people who lived in the houses or on the land before there were any buildings here. I saw a few native Americans and people dressed in early 1800s attire, as well as Confederate and Union soldiers and nurses.

The location or structure does not need to be very old to have ghostly inhabitants. Although you'll probably have better luck in those locations given the longer length of time that people have lived there. It is more likely for a spirit to haunt a location that it last knew in life, so this could be its home or the spot where it died, or both.

We have an eleven-year-old little girl ghost in my house that died during the 1970s. The girl liked to give our visitors a shock by appearing as a solid person to them then fading out. I think she liked to play pranks. I contacted her and she knows she died, but she likes the house and feels comfortable there. I told the girl she could stay if she did not scare anyone else and she hasn't for over 10 years now. The same thing could happen in any home, so don't rule out newer structures.

Also check out parks, abandoned buildings, bridges, old hospitals, mental institutions, old jails and prisons, hotels, restaurants, railroad stations and tracks, churches, battlegrounds, old courthouses, old town squares, places where ghost ships have been seen (Florida is a good place) and ghost towns. Brick buildings seem to be good places to look for some reason. I recently found that the stateroom on a cruise ship we took to the Caribbean was haunted. The ghost made strange fluttering and whispering noises for two nights, then I saw a dark apparition walk across the room on the night before we went home. Even though the cruise ship is only eight years old, there have been thousands of people on and off the ship, so chances are that a few have died on it and on other cruise ships, too.

Indian burial grounds or sacred spaces may be tempting to investigate, but I prefer to leave them alone out of respect. However, if a house has already been built on the site and the owners are having problems, I do go to see if I can help. Sometimes communicating with the spirits can alleviate aggressive (Protective) activity. See ghost clearing techniques later in this book.

There are haunted places in every city, town, and county in the U.S., but the older sites seem to have more activity. I've also have good luck in Europe and the U.K. where the structures there are much older and they have a much longer history.

Be sure to be very safe and always take a flashlight, water, and a cell phone with you when ghost hunting. It is not a good idea to go to a scary place alone so always take at least one buddy with you.

CHAPTER 9

The Investigation Process

1. Interview Witnesses
2. Rule out Other Possibilities
3. Get Evidence of a Haunting
4. Complete your Report

Interview Witnesses

If you are doing serious ghost hunting and want to be very professional about it or plan to write an article or book about your experiences, one of the most important things you can do is to interview witnesses. Talk to people who are currently occupying a home or building, and see if you can locate previous owners as well. Talk to managers and employees if you can (on your dime). It's a nice gesture to take someone to lunch for the interview if you have time. This information will give you a good idea of what you are dealing with. Be sure not to lead the witness -i.e. make suggestions during the interview.

An example of a leading question would be: "Was the apparition you saw very dark and non-transparent?" Instead, ask "What did the apparition look like?"

Following are some questions I take with me on a clipboard when doing interviews. You might want to copy this and keep several copies with you at all times so you won't forget anything.

1.) What is your name (and other witnesses)?

2.) Address of this location:

3.) When did you first occupy this location?

4.) What types of paranormal activity have you witnessed here?

5.) Sounds: []Talking []Whispering []Footsteps []Singing []Typing []Bells []Door closing/opening []Yelling []Crying []Other

____

6.) Smells: []Cigar []Pipe []Cigarette []Perfume []Cologne []Flowers []Foul odor []Firewood smell []Burning house []Other ____

7.) Taste: []Blood []Food []Other

____

8.) Do you know of any deaths that occurred here?

9.) Do you know the names of any deceased persons?

10.) Is the paranormal activity limited to certain areas?

11.) What unusual things have you seen?
[]Fog []Mist []Orb(s) []Lights []Full apparition(s)
[]Partial apparition(s) []Solid person []Person faded/disappeared
[]Other____

12.) If voices are heard, are they []male []female []child []baby

13.) Have you seen any animal ghosts?

14.) Have you had any UFO sightings in this area?

15.) Have you had any UFO encounters?
(People who have had UFO sightings often also have "haunted" houses)

16.) Have you witnessed any objects moving? []dropping []thrown []levitating []pulling covers off people []Other ________________________________

17.) If so, what were the objects?

18.) Were any of the movements threatening to any member of the family?

19.) Has anyone been physically touched by a ghost?

20.) If so, who was touched and what happened?

21.) Has anyone felt: []a change in temperature in any location []hotter []colder []cold chills/goose bumps []something moving through them []other

____

22.) Has activity increased over time?

23.) Do your guests/clients notice anything abnormal, or do things happen only around the occupants?

24.) Is there any history about this place? []Fire []Murder []Other

____

25.) Do you know of any graveyards nearby?

26.) Do you feel a sense of []Calm []Dread []Fear []Uneasiness []Curiosity []Anger when ghosts are around?

27.) Are you or is anyone in your family psychic?

28.) If so, have you ever seen ghosts at other locations?

29.) Does activity heighten around any certain time or event?

30.) Has the paranormal activity caused you to
[]lose sleep []want to move away []stay away as long as possible doing other activities []divorce your spouse []argue

31.) Have any ghosts followed you *to* other locations?

32.) Do you think the ghost(s) followed you *from* another location?

33.) Have you had ghostly activity at other locations you have lived/worked?

34.) Have any spirits been physically violent?

35.) Do they play mischievous tricks like hiding objects and returning them later?
[]Keys []Jewelry []Watches
Other____

36.) Has anything disappeared from your home/business only to show up at a different location at a later date?

37.) Do any spirits answer you out loud when you ask questions?

38.) Have you heard any audible replies on a digital voice recorder?

38.) Have your utilities: water, electricity, or gas been affected?

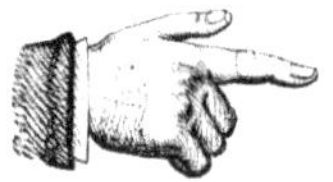

TIP:

Ask if there are any spirits present, who they are, and what they want. You can get most of the information you need with the answers to those three questions.

Rule out Other Possibilities

A professional ghost hunter will always rule out other possibilities for strange phenomena first. By being the skeptic, you will find that often a simple explanation can be found for many claims of hauntings.

Electrical Interference

EMF (Electro-magnetic field) readings can indicate the presence of a spirit. However, always check for obvious and hidden wiring, electrical junction boxes, and conduit that may be running through walls, under floors, or in ceilings. Check electrical switches and outlets, even if the owner believes they are disconnected. In several instances we have found old knob and tube wiring that was hot, even though the owners had the entire house rewired by an electrician. This can give you false positive readings.

Other items in the home that have electro-magnetic fields are electric blankets, alarm clocks, water bed heaters, cordless razors, computers, television sets, and cell phones, to name a few.

Also check outside the structure for nearby overhead or buried power lines or transformers. You'd be surprised how far away you can get EMF readings from these objects. Exposure to electro-magnetic fields is a controversial topic. Some scientists believe that EMFs are responsible for brain tumors, cancer, miscarriages and other health problems, as well as a cause of hallucinations. If you get high EMF readings above .05 mG, this may be a source to question.

A Gauss is a common unit of measurement of magnetic field strength. A Gauss (EMF) meter is an instrument which measures the strength of magnetic fields. Inside the Gauss meter there is a coil of thin wire. As a magnetic field radiates through the coil, it induces a current, which is amplified by the circuitry inside the Gauss meter.

Gauss meters can vary in the strength of the magnetic field they are capable of measuring. Since we are using a consumer grade EMF meter to help in our search for ghosts, the accuracy will not be that of a professional meter used by engineers, but will serve our purposes.

When ghost hunting, any EMF readings that occur away from electrical sources should be noted as possible evidence of a haunting.

Noise Sources

The most common complaint from people who think they have a haunted building is odd noises. The noises may sound like creaking floors and stairs, water dripping, scratching, banging, etc. The professional investigator will look for a natural explanation first such as leaking pipes, air in the water lines (this can be very loud), wind, heating/cooling vents that expand and contract when heated or cooled, and animals walking about the house. Wood stove pipes sometimes make noise when in use.

Also look for signs of rodents, squirrels, or raccoons, who can get inside the house through small holes, or under eaves and through chimneys. A common place for squirrel nests is in the attic. Raccoons, bats, squirrels, insects and chimney swifts find that chimneys are an ideal home for them, and we often find that these creatures can make a great deal of noise.

Note: have the homeowner call a licensed animal removal company to get rid of pests—never attempt this on your own. Animals carry rabies and other diseases that you don't want to be exposed to. Also never open a damper to investigate a chimney— you could expose yourself to carcinogenic soot and dangerous disease carrying bird droppings, etc. Not to mention that a live animal could come through the damper into the house.

Light Sources

If the occupant is seeing lights at night, see if you can visit at the time they experience it so you can see what the lights look like. Car headlights are the most common source, but train lights, reflections in windows, helicopters, lighted signs, and street lights should be investigated.

Hallucinations

Although we have rarely encountered a client who hallucinates, you cannot rule out the possibility. Certain medications, some illegal drugs, and some mental conditions may cause hallucinations. Since we are not trained in mental health we never mention this to the client. However, there are some cases where this might be the source of ghost sightings, especially if there is no other evidence and no other witnesses.

Psychic Awareness

I mention this because we have encountered several clients who are very psychic, but had absolutely no training in the area, and had no idea how to handle what they were seeing. Some psychics do not have the ability to turn their third eye (psychic center) off and on at will. They need to gain control of this and get training from another experienced psychic in order to deal with it.

One of the clients I worked with was very psychic and was seeing elementals around her house but had no idea what they were and thought they were ghosts. The elementals were tree spirits and possibly fairies. They moved about the inside and outside of the home as a tiny ball of bright white/blue light. Sometimes they would manifest in the form of a tiny person. I found that case highly unusual, since most psychics work for years to get to the level of

Pranks

If you do not find evidence of a haunting, consider that the source may be a prank by other people living in the house, or from neighbors, friends, etc. A case I worked on many years ago turned out to be a teenager in the neighborhood who threw rocks at the house at night after the husband left for work. This is always a possibility. After your ghost-hunting session if you want more information about the location that the homeowner can't provide, do research on your own. Libraries usually have micro-film of local newspapers and civil records offices will have copies of deeds and plat maps that may be useful. Also be sure to check old obituary pages for information about the deceased if applicable.

Your county Historical Society may have records that are not available elsewhere, and of course, the internet is a good resource, especially for news articles that are fairly recent. I've also used Ancestry.com for many of our investigations because they have access to many online resources such as military records and census records, however, there is a fee to join.

Steps of The Investigation Process

1. Do a clearing and protection session using a pendulum, crystal, meditation or affirmations before entering the property.

2. Discuss the haunting with witnesses and fill out the interview form.

3. Survey the grounds during daylight hours if possible to get a feel for the area first, especially if going into an unfamiliar location. Check for hazards like holes in the ground, rocks, etc. that could cause someone to trip or get injured. Mark these areas with a flag or other item that will be noticed.

4. Check for possible normal explanations for activity, sounds, or lights during the day and again at night. Check electrical lines and devices for abnormal EMF readings, check water pipes, pets, wind, open windows, air conditioner or heating vents.

5. Assign jobs and set up equipment on the site. I like to use as much wireless equipment as possible to avoid tripping on wires and the hassle of plugging in equipment in people's homes. We send people out in groups of two so that on one is alone, for safety, and also if something does happen worth noting there is another witness in the same location.

6. Do a walk-through each room with audio and video recorders, ask questions and wait for answers. Be patient. Ask if there are any spirits present, who they are, and what they want. Basically, you can get most of the information you need with those three questions. Take lots of photos.

7. If you feel cold spots or have other indications of a presence, ask the ghost to move a ball or pencil or other object, or make a noise to indicate their willingness to communicate. Ask yes or no answers, and ask the spirit to answer "yes" by moving an object. If that doesn't work, ask questions with a recorder on to check later, or leave the recorder on all the time to catch answers.

8. Do a trance session with a medium if possible to get more infor-

mation. Detailed answers may be obtained using this method. Mediums all work differently, so get familiar with how they like to work before having them go on an investigation with you. Some may do remote viewing and don't need to visit the site in order to gain information.

9. Tear down equipment and pack up. Do a second clearing and affirmation with the intention that all spirits will remain where they are now. The reason is that you don't want any pesky spirits following you home.

10. Check film and recorders for evidence after you are rested. Collect all of the evidence saved by each researcher.

11. If warranted, check civil records, newspapers, and libraries for more information about the location.

12. Make out your final report and keep a file of each of your investigations.

WARNING: Never take children or young teens on a ghost hunt. Children are more afraid of ghosts than they usually let on, and possession by an unfriendly spirit is more likely in children than adults. Possession is rare, but it is worth taking precautions against it to start with. Also some spirits have followed children home to haunt them instead of the people at the original place. When this happens it is usually a child ghost who wants a friend.

Paranormal Investigation Report

This report form is a sample of what I use in the field, then we enter the evidence into a computer that is used just for this purpose. Sometimes we take the computer with us in the field and one person does entry on site in order to save time. If you are very serious about ghost hunting, there are some programs available that will allow you to keep audio, video, and still photos in the report. In any case, keep some kind of record of your investigation for future reference and to provide the client. I keep a copy on a CD in case of a computer crash.

Date___________________
Site____
Owner ____
Address____
Phone___________________________Cell_________________
Emergency contact____
Time:_________________to______________________
Temperature outside: ______________ Inside:______________
Moon cycle: []Full []New []Waxing or Waning []no moonlight
Weather conditions: (wind, rain, snow, clouds, etc.)___________
____
Lead Investigator: ____
Investigators: ____
____
____
Guests: ____

Equipment used and investigator assigned:

Digital camera____
Video camera____
Night vision equipment___________________________________
Audio equipment____
Ambient Thermometer____________________________________
Laser Thermometer______________________________________
Infrared camera:____
Nigh Vision camera:______________________________________
EMF Meter: ____
White Noise: ____

Walkie-talkies:____________________________________
Other: ____

Unmonitored equipment set up and location:
Indoor motion-activated still cameras:__________________
Outdoor motion-activated still cameras: ________________
Remote wireless cameras connected to computer: __________

____
Computer (command center):__________________________
Other:____

Events experienced by each investigator: (describe in detail)
Lead Investigator:
Sound ____
Taste____
Touch/feeling___________________________________
Smell____
See____

____

Investigator 1:
Sound ____
Taste____
Touch/feeling___________________________________
Smell____
See____

____

Investigator 2:
Sound ____
Taste____
Touch/feeling___________________________________
Smell____
See____

____

Investigator 3:

Homeowner:

____

Investigator 4:
Sound ____________________________________
Taste_____________________________________
Touch/feeling_______________________________
Smell_____________________________________
See______________________________________
____

Homeowner:
Sound ____________________________________
Taste_____________________________________
Touch/feeling_______________________________
Smell_____________________________________
See______________________________________
____

Guest:
Sound ____________________________________
Taste_____________________________________
Touch/feeling_______________________________
Smell_____________________________________
See______________________________________
____

How to Get Rid of Ghosts

Before considering asking spirits to leave a place, think about what would happen if they were gone. Are ghosts good for business in a hotel or restaurant? If so, the owners may not want the spirits to leave. If the spirit likes being in a location, are they hurting anyone by being there? If not, maybe the best thing to do is to leave them alone. However, if the ghost is scaring people and you need to get rid of it there are a few methods that have worked well for me.

The first method is to simply ask the ghost to leave. That may sound too simple, but it usually works. You may want to talk to it and explain why by saying "You are scaring us (or the homeowner)," or "This is my house and I am not comfortable having you here.", then calmly ask it to go away. If this doesn't work right away, try talking in a firmer voice without yelling.

As I mentioned earlier, ghosts may not be aware that they are dead so you may have to explain to them that they are no longer part of the physical world and that they should look around for their spirit guide and move on towards the light. I close my eyes and visualize then going into the light. This method has been very successful for me. Some spirits are reluctant, but if you tell them that it will be better for them this way, they eventually move on.

If the spirit simply refuses, try suggesting to the occupants to not give it any attention or talking about it at all. This takes energy away from the spirit. Don't show any fear, because the energy of fear empowers negative spirits. Also tell homeowners to *not* use a Ouija board or have anything to do with the supernatural, which could open doors to the spirit world and allow the spirit more access during the time you are trying to get it to leave and until you are certain it is gone.

CHAPTER 10

How to Protect Yourself While Ghost Hunting

In order to protect yourself from mischievous or malicious spirits or worse, and psychic attack during ghost hunting you need to take several steps, some of which need to be done before arriving at the site you want to investigate. Do not forget this step or you could have some unpleasant experiences.

White Light

White light is used for protection by many people. First, get everyone together that is going on the hunt, preferably at a meeting place that is not near the site or at the least before entering the site. Have everyone form a circle and visualize white light above, below, and all around them, forming a protective cocoon of light. White light repels negative energies. Say the following or something similar out loud:

"I repel all negativity from us and this site we are about to visit and call in protective white light to surround us."

You may want to repeat this several times.

Upon arrival at the site or after your ghost hunt, you may want to get out your pendulum and do a clearing while visualizing white light (see the dowsing chapter). If at any time during the investigation process you feel threatened, take out your pendulum and do a clearing or repeat the white light protection method.

Some people carry clear quartz crystals with them on ghost hunts, since they carry high energy that negativity can't stand to be around. You might want to wear a crystal pendulum necklace or just carry one in your pocket. You may also charge a particular crystal for protection (see next page).

Wear Black

Another method of protection is to wear black. This may sound like the opposite of what you would expect, but black is a very powerful repellant of negative energy and also gives you more power. Black obsidian works well, too, if carried on your person. If you are doing a lot of ghost hunting, you may want to further protect yourself by keeping crystals in your house all of the time to repel any energies that you might accidentally bring back with you.

Although it is unusual for an entity to follow you home, it can happen. This usually happens to the inexperienced investigator. If you suddenly notice that you are feeling unwell, have extreme fatigue, or poltergeist activity in your house, do an immediate clearing of your home and do the white light visualization daily until you feel better.

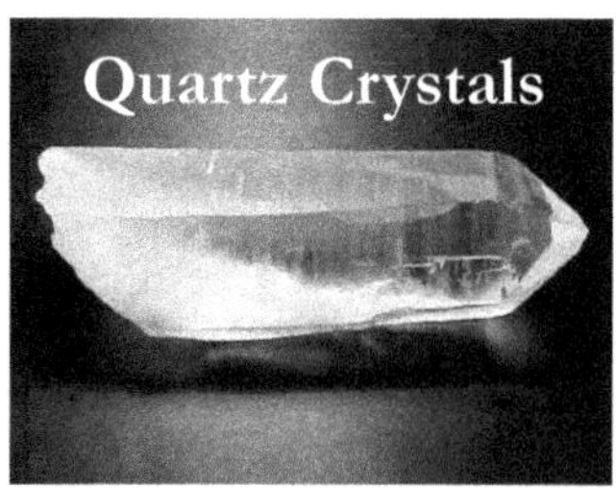

It is a good idea to keep a quartz crystal with you for protection, however, it should be cleansed and charged first. Choose a crystal that is a size you can easily carry. You may also want to have extra crystals or clusters in your home to use for protection 24 hours a day.

Obtaining Crystals

I go to Arkansas once a year to dig for my own crystals. It is a very inexpensive way to get your own crystals and assure that they have never been used by others. For a small fee, you bring your own bucket and tools with you to dig in the clay for crystals. Some mines allow you to go to the mine location, and others allow you to dig in piles they bring up for you. We go to the Ron Coleman Mine where the crystals are dug up with bulldozers and placed on the ground at the top of the hill so it is easier to access.

Be sure to wear old clothing and shoes since the red clay stains easily. Bring a crowbar, claw hammer, and a sledge hammer if you are ambitious. I bring my husband with me to do that hard work. You will find small crystals, small and large clusters, and big crystals. Sometimes there are crystals in plain sight, but most of the time you need to dig into the clay with your hands in order to feel them. Wash them off with the water nearby, or take along an extra bucket of water to rinse them in. You are allowed to stay all day to dig for one price.

I have found lots of crystals that I use to place around my entire house inside and out for protection. I also use some for communicating with spirits.

Cleansing a Crystal

I use two methods to cleanse. Either leave the crystal in a bowl of sea salt, Kosher sea salt for one week, or rinse it under cool spring water—preferably under a waterfall, but if none is available use spring water from a jug. This process removes any energies that the crystal may have picked up on its way to you.

Charging a Crystal

Charge crystals with the task you wish to use them for better results. Charge a clean crystal by holding it upside down with the bottom of the crystal in the palm of your hand. Now visualize white light energy coming through the top of your head, down your arm, and into the crystal, charging it along with the message to protect you at all times, or to help you communicate with spirits, etc. Do this for several minutes while you are in a quiet place with no interruptions. Stop when you feel that the crystal is fully charged. Only use the crystal you have charged for one purpose. Label your crystals If necessary to keep them separate.

Now keep the crystal in a bag in your pocket or around your neck as a necklace. You may make it into a piece of jewelry if it is the right size and wear it that way. I wire-wrap some of my crystals, which also double as an emergency pendulum for cleansing an area if needed.

Periodically re-cleanse and re-charge your crystal and only use this particular crystal for one purpose—protection. You may charge other crystals with different intents (such as communication) if you wish.

Using Crystals

To use clear quartz crystals for protection from psychic attack, keep one on your person at all times. Take along a crystal pendulum to use as a clearing device when you encounter negative energies at a haunted site. See the section on dowsing for tips on clearing with a pendulum. Finally, place crystals or clusters around your home and in your vehicle for 24 hour protection. The dark does not like the light in crystals.

To use a crystal for communication purposes, hold it in your hand and concentrate on the crystal and the spirit you wish to talk with. The communication will usually be telepathic rather than audible, however, keep the digital recorder on because sometimes EVPs come through during communication sessions.

Obsidian

One of my favorites, obsidian is a black smooth volcanic glass stone that is known for its protective qualities. I prefer to keep a 3" diameter round obsidian stone in my house and periodically cleanse it with sea salt. The obsidian stone has the unique quality of absorbing negative energy and keeping it in its external energy field until it is cleansed. Negative energy is drawn to it like a magnet, keeping the negativity away from you or others in the house. To cleanse, simply place the rock in a bowl of sea salt for two days, or wash under running spring water. When you sense that it is clear of any negativity, put it back in its regular place.

I also carry a small obsidian with me when doing any kind of investigation work for extra protection. Between my all black clothes, crystal necklace, and the black obsidian, I don't think its possible for anything negative can get through!

Other stones that are commonly used for protection and usually worn in the form of jewelry are Hematite, Black Tourmaline, Tiger Iron, Bulls Eye Agate, Rainbow Obsidian, Carnelian Agate, Ruby, Andulasite, Blue chalcedony, and Silver. See the next page for a listing of the most common stones used for protection purposes.

Stones With Protective Qualities

Agate: Protects against the Evil Eye
Amber: Protection from evil
Aquamarine: Protects sailors at sea
Blue chalcedony: Protects against evil magic, evil spells
Fluorite: Psychic protection
Hematite: Protects the warrior
Labradorite: Protects the aura from energy leakage
Obsidian: Absorbs negative energy
Malachite: General strong protection
Mother of Pearl: Protects newborns
Peridot: Protects the entire body, demon protection
Ruby: Protects family and possessions
Red Jasper: Protects in dangerous situations
Riverstone: Burial and building protection
Silver: Protects for evil spirits
Smoky Quartz: Protects from negativity in healing work
Sunstone: Protects from destructive forces
Tourmaline: Black, is a powerful protector
Turquoise: Protects from injury
Zircon: Protects from bodily harm

For more information on stone properties and uses, search the stone's name on the web.

Encounters with Negative Entities

There are negative spirits, just as there are negative people. I believe that the best practice is to leave them alone unless you have strong psychic abilities, a strong will, and proper training to confront these beings such as an expert like John Zaffis, nephew of the famous Ed and Lorraine Warren. Negative spirits and entities feed off of fear. They get their power from the power you give them unknowingly. If you can't face a negative entity without having fear about it—the best advice I can give you is don't do it.

I have faced several negative beings but the second experience I had was the most impressive. I'll share it with you so you can see how I handled it. I was 24 years old at the time and had been studying what most people would consider to be metaphysical subjects for several years. My father taught me several techniques for when I ran into something evil—which he assured me I would experience at some point in my life due to the fact that I am psychic. People who have their third eye open are subject to attack if they are not fully protected.

I played in a local rock band for over a year, then left after the leaders, a man and wife, asked me to participate in a bizarre act. I really had no idea up to that point that these two were anything but average normal people, but it turned out that wasn't the case. In fact, they told me that they had the lead singer involved, too. I finally realized that I had been lured into a situation by persons more experienced in the esoteric and who followed a different, more sinister path. With my eyes wide open now, I could see these people for what they were—a couple of witches who practiced black magic. They didn't want me to leave for two reasons—and one was because they were losing their bass player. The other was because I wouldn't let them take my energy. Both of them got very upset with me.

One evening a couple of weeks after I quit the group, my brother and I were sitting in the living room when we heard shaking objects in the kitchen, then the lights went off and on by themselves. I knew something was up, so I decided to go to my room and meditate on what it could be. I sat on the bottom edge of my waterbed facing my dresser and mirror, then lit a candle. A few seconds later, the window started shaking violently then flew open, blowing the drapes in. Then, the most bizarre thing—the water bed started jumping up and down with me on it! Now when filled with water the bed weighed at least a thousand pounds, so this was really impressive. I thought I was involved in remake of the Exorcist. Remembering what my father taught me, I resolved myself to confront whatever it was with absolutely no fear because I knew that was the only way to approach the situation.

I looked into the mirror on my dresser and saw—to my horror and amazement—the man who was the leader of the band. He acted surprised that I could see him. I gathered all of my strength and said very firmly and loudly "I know who you are and what you want. But you don't know who *I* am. You will leave now and not return ever again." I said this in a very threatening manner with all the power I could muster. His face faded away and the bed and window stopped moving. My brother came rushing into the room, wondering what the loud noises were and I told him, "Oh, I just got rid of a witch." That band leader never bothered me again.

I've confronted evil spirits at other times, and always did so without fear and having total confidence in my ability to stop whatever they were trying to do. There are people in this world and beings not of this world that will try to take advantage of the powers of an inexperienced psychic. When you are open to other worlds, you are open to everything, not just the good stuff. Fortunately, most of the time things are greatly exaggerated in the movies and they don't describe the real world. Most beings are just like you and me and not evil or negative.

CHAPTER 11

Real Ghost Hunts

Hill Park Cemetery in Independence, Missouri where Frank James and his wife, Ann Ralston are buried along with two Civil War soldiers and members of the Hill family.

Following are some accounts of ghost hunting investigations completed by the QUEST Investigation Group team, and my own experiences in some of the houses I've lived in. All of my houses have been haunted—you might say that *I'm* haunted. This is something I hear a lot from other psychics, too, so I've come to the conclusion that most houses do have spirits.

My Haunted House

Naturally I can't print the address here or we'd have tourists stopping by every day— but my home is located in an older section of Independence, Missouri. The house is 2500 square feet and consists of an older portion that was built in 1929 and a newer, larger addition that was built in 1986. We did extensive remodeling of the house which included removal of walls and relocation of the lower level bathroom, the addition of a dormer, and expansion of the kitchen. The original floor plan is pretty much the same, however, plus the addition.

From the time we moved in this house in 1987 until the year 2000, my husband and I operated a service business out of our home and had a secretary come in every weekday. The older front living room was converted to an office. My two daughters, ages ten and eight at the time, first brought ghostly activity to my attention when they reported hearing footsteps on the staircase to their bedroom. Sure enough, we heard a man's heavy stomping with boots, and a woman's lighter heels on the steps. When people visiting heard the steps and asked about it we said "Oh, that's just one of the ghosts." I decided to do a "scan" on the house to see if I could pick up anything else, and I sensed the presence of several adults and a little girl. None of them felt threatening, so we decided to leave the ghosts alone.

In September of 1988 the paranormal activity picked up. During a Girl Scout sleepover at our house the ghosts apparently decided to have some fun scaring the kids. They made noises on the stairs, in the walls and in the basement under the front living room where most of the girls were sleeping.

None of the girls slept very well and they couldn't wait to leave in the morning.

The next day five girls were still in the living room/office when I asked my oldest daughter where my keys were. She and I were standing about three feet apart. The keys lifted up off of a file cabinet where I had just looked, floated in the air a distance of five feet to a spot right between us at eye level, then dropped to the floor. All of the girl scouts saw this happen and ran - screaming— out of the house. They waited outside for their parents to pick them up. Of course, none of them would visit again. Now I knew I was dealing with at least one prankster spirit and did not appreciate it.

In January of 1989 I hired a new secretary (the first one quit due to paranormal activity while I was gone) and told her about the ghostly activity that had happened in the past but that it was pretty quiet now. She did not seem alarmed. I felt that I should tell her about it up front so she wouldn't be afraid if anything did happen. Not more than two weeks later I had to leave to do errands and came back to find my secretary wide-eyed and packing up her things. When I inquired as to why she was leaving she explained that she heard a noise in the basement and called out to see if it was my husband, Gene. When no one answered, she thought that he might be hurt and went downstairs to investigate. No one replied, but she did see a little girl (about age 11) with long blond hair in a white long nightgown standing by the furnace. When she asked if the little girl was ok, the girl slowly faded away and disappeared. I could not convince my secretary to stay after that incident.

I did another scan of the house and saw the little girl. She told me that she died in the house and it was because of the furnace. I did research but could find no reference to this incident. The only thing I could figure was that it may have been Carbon Monoxide poisoning due to a faulty heat exchanger or blocked flue.

I asked the neighbors in the area if they knew anything about the history of the house and found out that there were eleven people living in the house just prior to us. Since the room addition was incomplete, there was no heat or cooling in that part of the house so they must have all lived in the older, smaller side. That would have been very crowded. The neighbors reported that they heard a lot of fighting and yelling on several occasions, and that one or two of the men used to stomp up and down the stairs quite often. I also found out that a young girl was found dead in the house in the 1960s or 1970s.

In the summer of 1990 the ghost became audible. I was cleaning up the kitchen while my daughter, M. and her friend Jennifer washed and dried the dishes. Our house had not yet been remodeled in the kitchen and the old original cabinets were still in place. The bottom drawer often stuck so I told my family to always leave it open slightly so we could get it open more easily. On this occasion, I went to the drawer and it was tightly closed, so I said, "Alright, who closed this drawer?" To which a man's deep voice replied, "I did." The girls and I looked at each other, dumbfounded. We questioned each other as to who made that remark, and we decided that I would ask the question again. while we watched each other. I asked, and this time the ghost answered in a very annoyed manner. The reply was a louder male voice saying "I DID!" That was the last time that Jennifer visited us. I wish I had that on tape.

Not long after the kitchen episode, a ghost appeared in the window one evening. I drove up to the house after an outing with my daughters and as we pulled up to the side of the house a man pulled back the drapes and looked out of the window at us. We thought it was a burglar and went next door to call the police, who found nothing when they arrived. The doors and windows were all locked. My daughters and I stared at each other, knowing immediately that it was a manifestation of one of our spirits.

In 1991 I finally did a clearing of the house because one of the male spirits seemed to be gaining in strength and negativity. He did things to scare my daughters such as morphing posters of rock stars on the walls in my oldest daughter's room into hideous creatures. After my daughter complained of this, I watched one evening and witnessed it myself. I removed the poster and replaced it with another but the same thing happened. She also said she saw a dark figure floating around the room at night. I began to see evidence of something draining energy from both of my daughters because they seemed tired all the time and suspected that it was he. My daughters had not yet learned how to protect themselves fully against psychic attack and it was evident that something needed to be done.

I will not go into how the clearing was done here because it can be a very dangerous procedure if not done correctly and by an experienced psychic. Suffice it to say that the negative spirit is gone, along with the other adult ghosts in the house.

The little girl has since appeared to us several times. She starts out as a white mist, then materializes fully except for her feet. She always wears a white long nightgown and floats in the air. The spirit can answer us by closing the basement door or knocking on it or something else in the basement. We feel her presence often. I have asked her if she would like to go to the light and get on with the next world, but as of 2006 she is not ready to go yet. It seems that she has a strong attachment to the house. Since she is doing no one any harm I will leave her alone for now.

The Portal

We have a portal located inside and outside the house on one exterior wall off of the deck. This portal appears at times in the shape of a round swirling hole and at other times as a four-pane

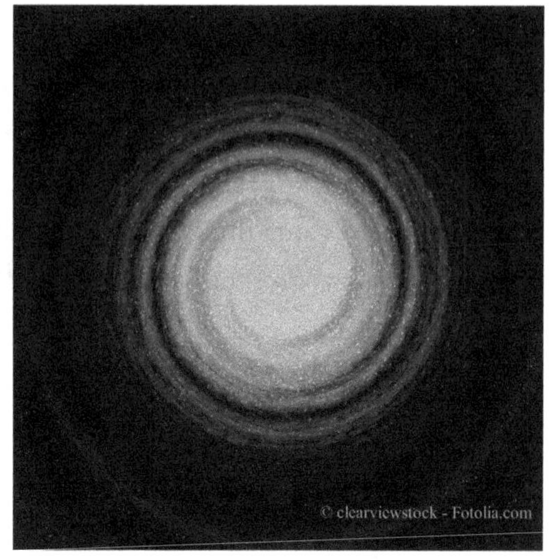

window that I and my oldest daughter and other researchers can see. I was surprised to find that this type of portal appears to other people as well and has been photographed. We have not been able to get any photos of our portal yet. It used to open regularly in the fall each year and stay open for a few days or weeks at a time, but recently has been open all year-round.

During the time that this portal is open we may see spirits appear to go in and out of it. Often, these entities don't seem to notice me or anyone else and just pass through the portal and move through our yard to go on about their business somewhere. Sometimes, whatever comes to our world does seem to be observing me and/or my family. I am at a loss to explain why the portal is in that particular location, when it first appeared, or why it is there. Maybe it has always been there—even before the house was built. I have observed the portal on several occasions and it may be that this is how beings and spirits from other dimensions travel back and forth to this dimension.

Summer 1988: My husband and I were gone to work and one of my daughters was playing with two friends, a boy and a girl. The house was dimly-lit as all of the windows were covered with aluminum foil to keep out the hot sun. The kids were running through the house, playing chase, but when they came to the stairway in the new addition of the home, they came to an abrupt halt. They saw a face on the wall at the foot of the stairs. It was about three feet high, and at first it reminded them of a skull as the eye-sockets were solid and large, but were odd-looking; and it appeared to wear a helmet. There was no explanation, no source of light to have caused it. They ran from the house and didn't stop until they were down the block. They were scared, and couldn't figure out how it got there, and even more, they'd never seen a face like that. Later, my daughter saw a new book I had purchased lying on the table. She screamed, "that's the face!" It was Communion, by Whitley Strieber (1987).

The face has never reappeared, but a silvery mist has appeared in the same location several times. I suspect that whatever it was it came through the portal, which is approximately 20' from that spot.

October 2004: At a Halloween party in 2004 I asked a friend of mine, Chris Brethwaite, a paranormal investigator in the Kansas City area, if he could sense where a portal might be in the house. I told him nothing else. He found the spot within two minutes. Chris said he could feel a difference in the air and that it felt like a vacuum. He could not see it, but definitely knew where it was. I then asked another psychic friend of mine to come in the room and he located it in the exact same position. He also reported a vacuum like feeling when he placed his hand in the area.

October 2005: While my husband was out of town on his annual fishing trip with his dad I stayed home to run the business. On Sunday evening I took the trash out to the curb for the Monday morning pickup and when I returned to the deck on the side of the house there was a large black creature sitting in the middle of the deck. It had the head and upper body of a very large cat or small panther and the lower body and tail of a possum. I estimate that it was approximately thirty inches in length, not counting the tail. I thought for a moment that this was an actual animal. It looked at me, then ran down the steps of the deck to the driveway and disappeared into thin air. I am sure this was a creature who entered from the portal.

September 23, 2006: I went out to the hot tub for my nightly spa (a necessity for people who work long hours) and almost immediately noticed a large eye, complete with detailed eyelid, pupil and iris at the portal area. It simply looked at me for a while then disappeared. I closed my eyes for a minute, then opened them again and saw a white rod shape about 6-8" in length over the sliding glass doors to the right of the portal area It stayed for one second, then darted into the wall over the doors. I got the distinct feeling that it was observing me. Obviously, the portal continues to open.

We have wood lattice work around our deck and I have noticed that while meditating I can see into another dimension by looking through the lattice. So far, I can only do this at night. I have seen other people and animals walking or moving about that seem oblivious to me. Sometimes I see eyes of different creatures looking in at me as if they are looking through a window. At times a whole face will be visible and sometimes they are not human. I have asked my guides what these creatures are and found out that they are 5th and 6th dimensional beings that share the same location as we do but because of their high vibration we do not normally see them. They are simply observing me when I observe them, but normally they do not watch what I or anyone else does. I catch a glimpse of these entities while in a meditative state, but not when I am going about my normal daily business. I have no reason to disbelieve them, but I am still cautious.

Aliens or Ghosts? August 29, 2006: My husband went out of town on an annual fishing trip and I was home alone. I should note here that most unusual events happen to me when he is not in the house. One evening, I was awakened at 3:00 a.m. to a loud, clicking sound coming from the doorway in my bedroom. It sounded like it was approximately six feet up from the floor. I was immediately wide awake and knew that something was not right. The sound was a series of six clicks that sounded like an animal noise. Each click had a different tone and style. I knew somehow that this was a communication from one type of creature to another, but don't know why I know that. I felt the presence of two beings in the room and looked around but saw nothing. We have a skylight above our bed and the moonlight was adequate to see everything.

A few minutes later I heard someone walking on our gravel driveway, then the hot tub jets came on. Next, I heard a crash in the kitchen sink. Oddly, I fell back asleep when normally I would have turned on the light and gone downstairs to investigate something like that.

The next day I checked the sink and nothing was there. The cats were outside so they couldn't have made any of the sounds in the house. I called my daughters and found that they had experienced some very odd things the same night. My youngest daughter had a baby boy prematurely and he was still in the hospital. She had to pump milk every four hours to take to him and was up at midnight in her living room with the machine on when she heard a loud banging on the wall near the front door (This is our rental house on Pearl). It was a methodical banging and she thought someone must be playing a joke on her. She ran upstairs to see if either of her older two boys was kicking the wall. Both boys were fast asleep and not moving. The noise stopped when she left the chair, but she called her older sister anyway.

When her sister and brother-in-law arrived, they walked the perimeter then drove around the block and saw nothing. They headed back home, then the banging started up again. This time, and she called the police. Her sister also returned. No one, not even the police found anything. And the boys were still fast asleep. I did a reading on the house and could not determine the source of the banging noises—which is odd because I can usually pick up *something.*

Later that same night, my other daughter was awakened at 5:00 a.m. by a bright green light the size of a golf ball coming from the satellite receiver. Normally, the green light on the receiver is very tiny (1/4"), but it was very large and bright at this time, then it suddenly went back to normal size. She was now wide awake and she would normally be very groggy at that time of the morning.

This is similar to my feeling of being wide awake when I heard the sounds at 3:00 a.m.. Then she saw a blinding white light underneath her bedroom door, but when she got up to open the door there was nothing there and the white light was gone.

Why all three strange events occurred on the same evening, I do not know. But it's extremely bizarre.

September 15, 2006: Our phone goes out whenever it storms. Somehow water gets in the line and after a few days it dries out and comes back on. This time, however, the phone did not come on for over two weeks so I called the phone company, who said they would come out the next day. That evening, while I was in the house alone the phone rang twice with the rings being close together. Only one phone rang—the others did not. At first I thought the phone company had come early and fixed the line, but when I picked up the phone it was still dead. The next day, the technician came out and fixed it and said they had not been out before. I don't know why or how that phone rang, but it was during a television show I was watching on ghost hunters. Was it a message?

The next day the phone was out again. I called the phone company to ask if they could do a line check and they said that the phone was off because I ordered a disconnection. I did not call them and neither did my husband. Now I am trying an internet phone service and we'll see what transpires with that!

October 12, 2006: My husband fell asleep on the couch at 9:30 p.m. and I got in the hot tub outside on our deck. I felt as if something was watching me but all was quiet. My dog, Gracie, then started to jump on the wood gate to her kennel, frantically trying to get out. I looked over in that direction and saw an 8' tall human-looking dark figure walk from one side of the shed to the other and through the wood fence into Gracie's pen. (I know the height because I was able to measure a point on the shed the next day where the top of the head was located.) The dog immediately stopped barking and trying to get out. I was concerned that something hurt her and tried to get my husband to go investigate, but he wouldn't wake up. So I locked the doors and went to bed, hoping that whatever it was would go away. I believe this creature probably came from the portal.

January, 2007: I got in the hot tub at around 10:30 and immediately felt like I was not alone, although everything was very quiet. There had been a recent snow and ice storm in the area, so it was quieter than usual. I then heard a clicking sound coming from a few feet behind me in the driveway, but since the deck has lattice and solid walls around it I couldn't see anything. There were a series of 10-11 clicks of different tones, similar to the clicking I heard in my bedroom several months before. It sounded like the noise was coming from approximately 6' off the ground. I felt that the sound was some sort of communication between two beings.

I practically froze with fear, which is unusual for me. I sensed danger, and immediately went in the house without looking in the drive. Normally, I would have stopped to look to see what it was, but I knew deep in my soul that the creature that made that noise was not anything of this world.

August, 2007: On August 18, 2007 I was sitting on the porch at around 10:00 p.m. when I noticed a flash of light in the sky just above the trees in our back yard. It looked similar to lightning, but was a very small, thin, white line that measured approximately 2" across if I held something up to cover it at arm's length. There were no storms in the area. Intrigued, I continued to watch the area for more lights, and sure enough, during the 20 minutes I stayed on the porch, I saw multiple flashes of tiny electrical charges of varying lengths and flash times. The longest flash time was a full two seconds. This seems to be longer than normal lightning. The flashes of light appeared around and up to approximately 15' over the trees but no where else.

On August 19, I returned to the porch in the late evening once again and noticed tiny white flashes of lights—this time over a tree not 20' from the house. It appeared that they were very close to me and not something far away. They also kept close to the tree, and did not appear anywhere else. I continue to observe this nightly.

January, 2008: I was sitting in the living room watching TV and glanced up to see an apparition of a tall man walk in front of the living room door and head towards the laundry room. I jumped up to grab my Nikon camera that was sitting on the dining room table nearby and took some photographs. The camera would not work at

What appears to be a ghostly set of stairs that are not currently in the house.

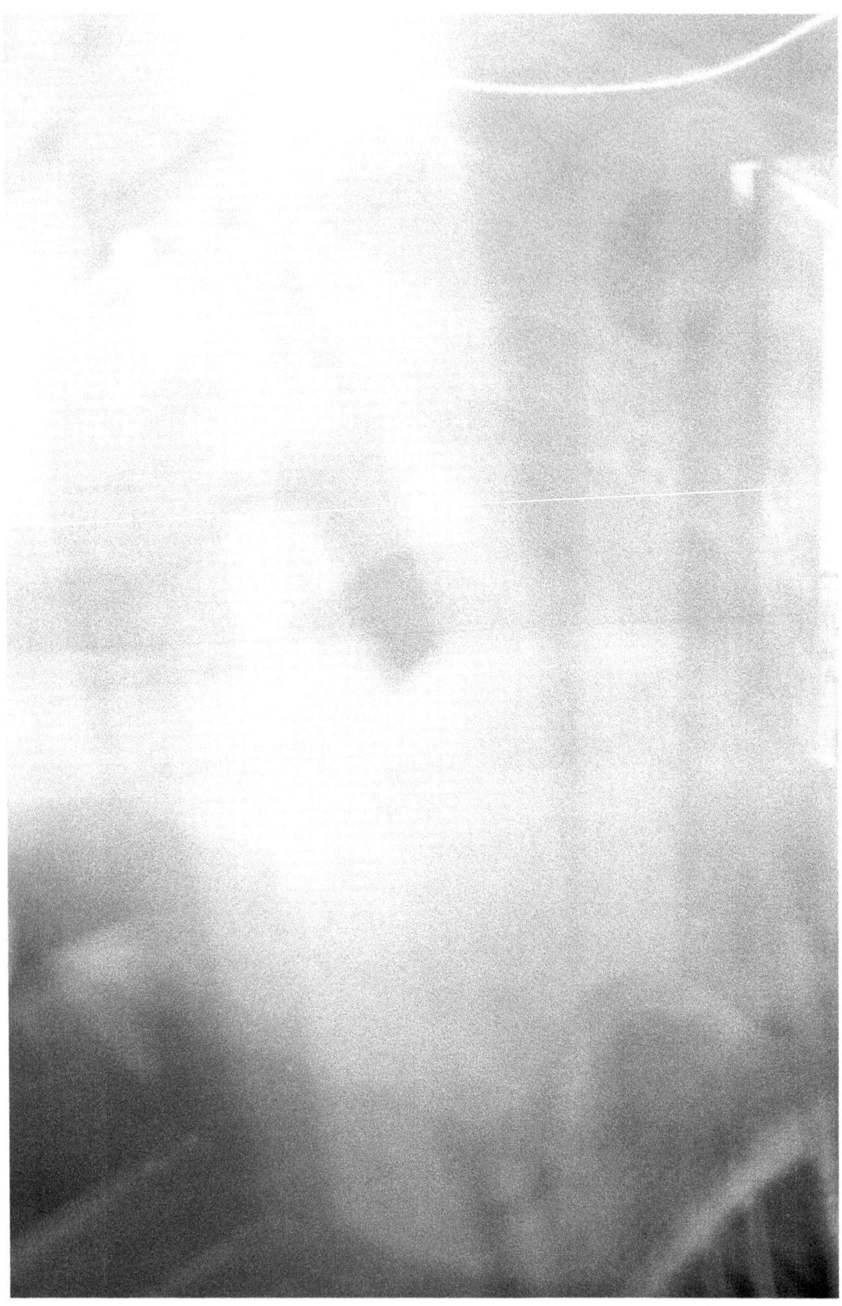

What appears to be a distorted hand in front of the camera lens, as if to try to stop me from taking a picture.

first (oddly) but after I took one picture of some flowers on the dining room table, I then took three more pictures in the direction of the laundry room. The camera was set to take three pictures in a row very quickly, so these were taken less then a second apart. The third photo (not shown) was completely whited out.

My Daughter's Haunted House

Pope Street house in Independence (now razed) was one of the most haunted locations I have experienced. The house was at least one hundred years old at the time of our visit. One of my daughters rented the home for a period of one year. She lived there with her husband and young son, and was pregnant with her second child.

Soon after moving in, she asked me to visit the house because she felt that it was haunted. She had already seen several apparitions and had poltergeist activity in the kitchen area. There was a water leak that started suddenly and she could not get it turned off; a large picture hanging began banging wildly against the wall and abruptly stopped. She also saw a window appear on a blank wall then disappear.

Right after I arrived to investigate, several dishes fell to the floor, even though no one was nearby. I felt the presence of several angry ghosts, so I went into trance to see who they were and what they wanted.

The first spirit was that of an older man named Peter, who built said he'd built the house. He felt very attached to it and felt that anyone living there was an intruder. I asked him if he knew that he was dead and he said yes but it did not matter, this was his house. Peter was the one making noises in the walls, turning water off and on in the bathroom and kitchen, and breaking dishes. I asked him if he was ready to leave and go to the light. He wanted to think about it and said he would talk to me if I came back later. I knew he was lying about wanting to talk to me again.

There were several other spirits at the location that were much older and had been there for hundreds of years—well before any houses were built in the area. They are settlers and Native Americans, and are protecting the location.

I then turned my attention to something else that caught my eye when I'd been speaking to Peter. I saw several small "people" that looked more like alien grays. They moved back when they saw that I could noticed them. It seemed as though they were very surprised that anyone could see them. I could sense that they were there to observe my daughter and when I asked about it they said yes, but it was none of my business, and to leave them alone because they had a job to do and they were not harming anyone.

After discussing this with my daughter, we used some techniques to protect her and her children. It worked, and she did not have any visits from the "aliens" or ghosts again. I drove past the location where the house was and still feel negative energy there. I think this may be a portal area where entities can come and go at will.

Crysler and Lexington Ghosts

There is a 100–year old+ house at the corner of Crysler and Lexington in Independence that was made into three apartments. There are two apartments on the lower level and one unit above them. This house is located on the exact spot where a civil war

battle was fought near a railroad cut in 1864. I was called to investigate paranormal activity in both lower level apartments.

I started my first investigation of this property on the right side apartment of the building. The tenant, C.C., told me that she saw a dark shadow in the shape of a man move across the living room/dining room area on several occasions during the day and night. She reported that she also heard scratching and banging in the wall behind her bed and in her bedroom closet. Her two small children refused to go near the closet and she had to get out their toys and coats for them when they needed them. C.C. said that the activity increased in frequency since she moved in a year earlier and that it felt more menacing as time went by.

Immediately upon entering the apartment I could sense a heavy presence that seemed to move around the room. I went into a trance and saw a man wearing a long black trench coat, pants and boots that looked like 1860s attire standing in the dining room area. He had an angry look on his face and was looking right at C.C. The

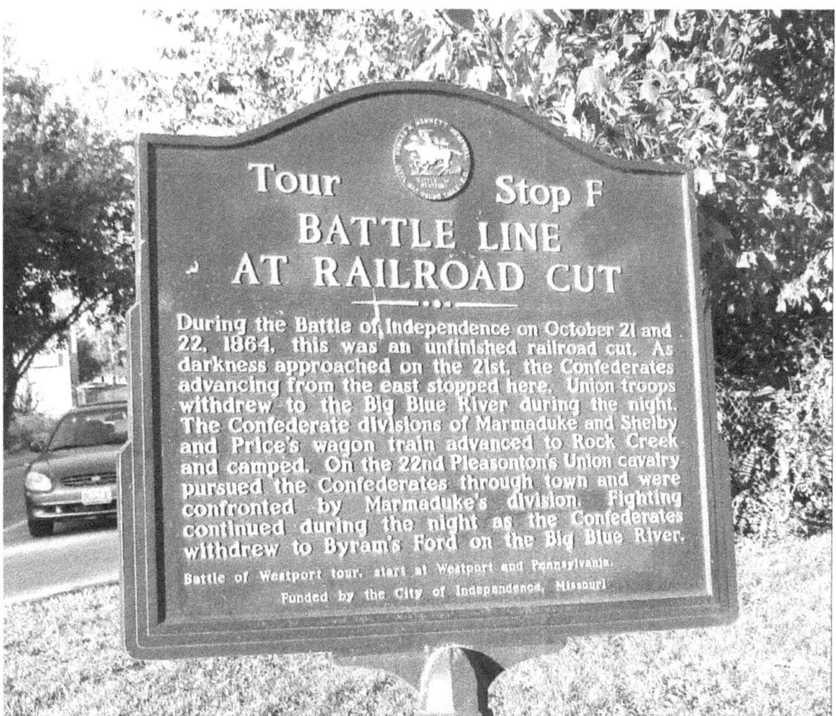

man said he did not want her or anyone else in this location because it belonged to him. He walked to the closet area. I could see that he didn't live in this house as it was, but lived at that location in a small cabin many years ago. The closet area was likely the original entrance to the log cabin and was where he walked in and out of this world. I did a clearing and afterwards, the spirit was quiet but he remained there.

I then visited the neighboring apartment to see C.C. who told me that she was experiencing banging noises in the wall adjacent to the right side apartment and heard loud footsteps in the vacant apartment above her. When she looked inside the upper level apartment there was no one there. She also saw her kitchen cabinet doors open and close on their own and saw a white shadow and a dark shadow on several occasions. C.C. said that the kitchen cabinets flew open and slammed closed, and dishes flew out of the cabinets and came crashing to the floor the night before my arrival, which is what finally prompted C.C. to call me.

After going into trance I saw the same man from the right side apartment passing through, and also a petite woman. The woman had no relation to the male entity and had died recently. She told me that she was trying to get C.C.'s attention because C.C. is psychic. She wanted help of some kind because she felt wronged. I was able to see what she needed help with, but we were unable to assist her.

I visited the apartment at a later date to do a clearing, which was unsuccessful. This happens when an entity is very strong-willed and thinks they have unresolved issues that must be taken care of before they move on. In this case, her spirit is unwilling to leave until things are resolved to their satisfaction.

Both tenants moved out after their leases were up due to ongoing paranormal activities at their apartments.

During a recent visit to the property, I went in to a trance state and saw several civil war encampments in the area with men in confederate uniforms. There were teepees of guns next to tents and burning fires with cooking utensils all around. I saw the men fire their guns, and noted that I could see flame come from the end of the guns when they were fired. The noise was deafening. I could see men on both sides get injured and fall. I saw injured men being carried away on stretchers and loaded into horse-drawn carts. They were headed to a nearby hospital, which was a large home that had been converted.

The soldiers fired across the railroad cut, which was unfinished at the time. There was intense and continuous fighting and many spirits still roam the area. It was extremely difficult to see the pain and suffering these men endured and I had to leave after a short time.

There is a place to stop next to this location on the west side of the corner where the marker is located. If you like, step out of the car and walk around the area and see if you can feel or see anything. I think this would be an excellent place to ghost hunt because of the extreme emotion that is left behind after a battle.

Rose Hall

Rose Hall is a Jamaica plantation in Montego Bay. It is reportedly haunted by the White Witch of Rose Hall, the hundreds of slaves she killed there, and three of her husbands. I visited the site in 2006 while in port on a cruise.

Annie (or Rosa) Palmer was born in England to an Irish father and English mother but spent most of her life in Haiti. After her parents died she was adopted by nanny who taught her witchcraft and voodoo. Annie moved to Jamaica and married John Palmer, who owned Rose Hall Plantation. Annie murdered Palmer, two later husbands and numerous male slave lovers. She was then murdered by a slave named Takoo.

The guides tell of a horrible pit where Annie would through slaves in to die of starvation and thirst if they did anything to make her mad. A mirror on the wall of her bedroom will reportedly show her ghost if you take a photo of it.

Mirror that Annie appears in

Mound Grove Cemetery Encounters

Some people would say we are nuts for visiting graveyards on Halloween night, and they may be right, but what better time to see ghosts that might be lingering? The reason we investigated this location was because of an incident that a certain teenage girl had there, several years earlier.

She was sixteen years old and just had a fight with her boyfriend. She decided to drive to the Mill Creek Cemetery to be alone and think. So for whatever reason, she got out of her car and walked through the cemetery at—yes– midnight.

She found a nice spot next to a tree and sat down. She was approximately 200 yards from the front gate. No one else was around (who would be?) and it was a very quiet, moonlit night. She closed her eyes and meditated for a few minutes. The thought occurred to her that up to this point she had never actually seen a ghost, although people around her could and she felt somewhat jealous of them. She thought "What better time and place to see a ghost?" and said out loud, "If there is any such thing as ghosts, show yourself to me—right now!"

Right on cue, a white apparition appeared at the bottom of the hill. The girl couldn't believe it, but she stood up and stared at it to be sure. It moved towards her. Now she could see that this was the apparition of a woman wearing a long white gown. She had no feet and glided through the air. Panicked, the girl started running to her car. She kept running and glancing back, only to see that the spirit moved faster towards her. Finally reaching the car, she looked back and the ghost slowly faded away at the edge of the cemetery. It seemed she could not go past the gate.

Location where the dark shadow of a man appeared, answered me, and walked towards us.

Spot where the teenager sat when she saw the floating lady. Note the streak across the front of the tombstone of a woman–could it be the ghost?

Our team of five decided to see if we could get the lady ghost to appear again so we could get her on film. We arrived at the cemetery at 11:00 p.m. and walked in through the front gate. We agreed to stay together at all times for safety. I started by filming the entrance and graves in the immediate area with my infra-red camera. Crewmember, Maria, took the digital camera and took several shots because we sometimes get orbs or spirits on film that are not visible to the naked eye. This evening, however, we saw a fog appear over some of the graves, and that was not visible on the film. But no apparitions made their appearance at that time.

We moved further into the park, and as we did so, it got darker since we no longer had the streetlights illuminating the area. The moon was out so that helped a bit. As our eyes became accustomed to the dark we could see better. After a while, I decided to stay behind with another crewmember, Donna, while the others, Maria, Rachel, and Jamyi walked further on their own. For some reason, we forgot all about our agreement to stay together—big mistake.

I looked around at some of the local gravestones and took notes. Donna and I felt the presence of a couple of spirits, but nothing materialized. I did some filming, and after what seemed like forty-five, I called out for the others. They did not answer. I walked a little way down the road where it was very dark, and called again. I heard Maria's voice answer me and saw what I thought was her dark, shadowy figure walking toward me on the small paved road. After a minute, the three women appeared at the top of the hill. I then realized that the black figure that had answered me was NOT Maria after all. I moved backward and told the three women to look at the bottom of the hill, and they all saw the dark apparition moving toward me. They froze and would not come forward. I moved quickly back up the other side of the hill from where I came, and when I looked back, the figure was gone. The five of us decided we'd had enough that night and left pretty quickly.

Note: the cemetery gate is now locked at night, so I wouldn't suggest an after-dusk visit.

Ghosts or Men in Black?

This is truly one of the strangest investigations I have ever done, and I think you'll find it extremely odd, too. In late summer of 2003 I received a call from a woman who was very panicked. She is a housewife, and lives with her husband and two dogs. In her 63 years she had never seen anything like this.

Sara D. was awakened at approximately 5:30 a.m. on a Saturday morning by her dog, who needed to go outside. It was still dark outside and it was unusual for the dog to wake up that early. Sara got up and let the dog out the front door, then waited for him on the font stoop. She looked across the street and noticed that there was a newer black four-door sedan parked in front of her neighbor's house two doors down and across the street. She thought it was odd that the parking lights were on. Sarah noticed a male driver and possibly a male passenger in the front seat of the car, both wearing dark clothes. The passenger turned around and looked directly at her, and Sara could see that he was wearing sunglasses.

Sara then looked at the house, expecting a person to come out of the door to the waiting car. Instead, she saw a small, 6" - 10" diameter bright white light pass through the closed door of the house, then travel to the waiting car and enter through the back passenger side window. Immediately, Sara saw a third person sitting in the back seat who wasn't there before. The car took off quickly. Sara said she could swear that the light became a person when it went into the car. She thought that the quick retreat from the house was a reaction to her watching the car.

I went to the location the next day and scanned the area to see what I could pick up. I did not feel the presence of any spirits in the house or see anything unusual at the time of my visit. I did, however, sense that the people in the house Sara mentioned were being watched, but by whom (or what) I could not tell. The black sedan, men wearing black suits and black sunglasses certainly fit the description of "Men in Black." I do think that Sara is telling the truth about what she saw. She and her husband have since moved away to another state and oddly, their house burned down while it was vacant.

Dark Spirits Haunt Family

Another house on the East Lexington block is haunted by unfriendly spirits. The family told me of events dating as far back as

1976 when J.D. and his wife, Bettie, moved in the house with their two young boys.

Not long after moving in, the entire family noticed that they felt like they were being watched all the time. None of them could explain it. While the husband and boys were away at work and school during the day, Bettie would notice this feeling more often. After a few months, Bettie noticed that things would get misplaced, only to turn up in an odd place. Keys would be missing from the key hooks by the door and turn up underneath a laundry pile. Her hair dryer disappeared one day, only to show up on the back porch a few days later. Her husband said that she must have moved these items and forgot about it but Bettie knew better.

In 1977, the youngest boy, age ten, started complaining that he was now afraid of the dark and would like a nightlight. This was odd since he had not been afraid of the dark before. He said he saw red eyes watching him at night. At first, the older brother did not believe him, but he soon started seeing the red eyes as well, and he too wanted the nightlight on. Soon that was not enough, and the boys started leaving on the table lamp. They were losing sleep because of the "monsters" in their bedroom.

Their father still did not believe that anything unusual was going on, and he did not experience anything unusual. Approximately two years after moving in the house, Bettie saw a Cheshire cat in the tree in their back yard. She thought it was her imagination at first and tried to ignore it. The cat looked like a cartoon cat with a big smile. It showed up on several occasions when she was alone, but would never appear when any one else was around. Bettie was afraid to hang her laundry outside anymore and asked her husband to purchase a dryer. He refused. She did not mention the cat for fear of sounding crazy.

As the years went by, the activity increased. Finally, all of the family members saw the red, glowing eyes and dark shadows in the upper bedroom that the boys shared. They all experienced hearing footsteps walk across the upper floor when everyone was downstairs. And everyone experienced missing items that would appear weeks or months later in odd places. An overwhelming feeling of negative energy in the house pushed the two boys to leave home because they could not stand to be in the house. As soon as they each turned eighteen, they moved out. The parents opted to stay and hoped things would return to normal, but they didn't.

Months would go by with no activity, but as soon as anyone noticed that things were quiet around the house, something new would happen. It was as if someone or something was listening and reacting to the conversations of the homeowners.

Our paranormal research team was called to investigate the house in 1999. We arrived at the house, but none of us could go inside except Maria. We all felt an overwhelmingly heavy, dark presence. I decided that we would do our investigation from another location and do remote viewing. 'Remote viewing' is a term for observing things from far away; whether it is a city block or around the world. This is a technique that I used often in my investigations to find missing persons. While none of the rest of our team had used the technique before, they all quickly learned how to do it.

We split up and I asked each team member to see what they could find out on their own. When we compared notes it was surprising even to us how similar our findings were. Each of us saw a dark entity that could materialize at will. None of us felt it was human, but that it was similar to 'shadow people', such as those outlined in *The Secret War* by Heidi Hollis (2008).

Shadow people are sometimes considered to be non-human entities that observe people and take energy from them. They can only live on fear generated by people, hence the menacing red eyes that would certainly scare anyone, especially a child. We all felt that the other paranormal activity in the house was generated by this dark presence that was growing in strength and also by several spirits of people who had passed on. I sensed that some of these were Native American spirits and they were angry about their land being disturbed.

I could only advise the family to leave the house as soon as possible as I had no experience getting rid of this type of entity. The house mysteriously burned down while the family was out of town in early 2006.

Note: I have observed two other shadow people in my lifetime. The first happened in 1978. It was in the shape of a man who stepped out of some trees while my husband and I drove through a neighborhood. The man walked to the center of the road, then disappeared in front of our eyes. The second incident was in May of 2006. I saw a man wearing an old western-style coat and low wide-brimmed hat standing on the steps of the First Presbyterian Church on Lexington. He was all black from head to toe. The man stood there for a minute while I was stopped at a stop sign, then disappeared. I was quite shaken up by this incident and it still bothers me when I pass by this church. After recently visiting Mount Grove Cemetery where Joseph Smith, III is buried, I feel that his ghost does haunt the place occasionally due to some unfinished business.

Rotary Park Encounters

Rotary Park is located one block south of 23rd Street, and few blocks west of Sterling in Independence, MO. It is a popular place for children to play and for adults to walk on the track around the park. There is a creek on the south and west side of the park and a big hill on the west side beyond the creek.

My eldest daughter and I used to take walks in the park almost nightly starting in the spring of 2003. We did not notice anything unusual about it until September, 2003 when the park cleared out earlier in the evenings and was fairly quiet. Often, we were the only two people walking. One evening while briskly walking along on the east side of the track I felt a shaking in my entire body that started at my head and jaw, then traveled downward. The shaking stopped when I moved forward. I stepped backward a few steps and the shaking started again. I could feel a definite difference in the air in this one spot. My daughter stepped into the space and said she felt an "electrical" type feeling.

The next evening we returned to the park again. The spot was still there and felt the same to me. I was intrigued about it and decided to go into trance to see what it may be. We sat on a park bench and suddenly I saw spirits all around the park. Some were Imprints, which are what I call *Imprints in Time* where a psychic can see events that happened in the past as if watching a movie. I saw small log cabins, several tent camps, lots of camp fires and many people milling about. A few of the apparitions were ghosts.

The first ghost is a man who hangs out around the south edge of the park. He looks like an old prospector and has a gold pan in his hand. He wears a dirty white shirt, suspenders, pants, boots and an old raggedy hat. I see a tent set up with a fire and pot in front of the tent facing the stream. The man means no one any harm, but he does not like it when people get too close to him. He seems not to realize that he is dead. There is an odd impression in the grass in this area where the grass blades move in the opposite direction of the wind at times. My daughter and I have noted this on several occasions. I believe that is where the man's tent was. The name he gave me is "Old George."

Another ghost is that of a young woman in her late twenty's or early thirties. She wears a long dress and stands next to a large tree on the west center side of the park near the walking track. This is a good place to visit if you really want to feel a ghost. If you place your hand on the east side of the tree 12" away from the tree approximately 5' up from the ground it will feel noticeably colder or warmer than the air around it. We took a tour to this park on Halloween night in 2004 and all eleven people could feel the spot next to the tree. Three could see a white mist in the same space. I can see a woman materialize there and then turn to white mist. She told me her name was *Anne*. She feels very attached to the location. When I did a reading of the area, I got the name of Frank James but did not know why there was a relationship to this woman.

I asked a history buff friend of mine, Joe Rudzik, about this location and he told me that where there is currently a brick schoolhouse at the top of the hill was a replacement for an older school. Frank James' girlfriend was the schoolteacher, and the original schoolhouse was in what is now Rotary Park. In those days it was customary for a teacher to be unmarried. When the community refused to let the woman marry Frank James and still retain her position as teacher, the school mysteriously burned down.

Frank then offered to rebuild the school but only if his new wife could continue to teach there. The town council agreed, and the new school was built. I think this woman is the ghost of Frank James' wife. I did research on the internet and found that her name was *Anna* "Annie" Ralston (1853-1944). Frank James (1843-1915) is buried in Hill Park, directly north across 23rd Street, and I Anna is buried with him. I believe her ghost haunts the park because she has a strong attachment to the school.

In October of 2007, I took a group of investigators to this park on two different nights. On both occasions everyone felt a difference in temperature next to the "Anne" tree and I was able to get several photos of orbs. One class attendee had is video camera battery suddenly go from 1 hour time left to 45 seconds in an instant. He was standing near the tree when it happened. Also at the same instant, I saw Anne come out of the tree. Perhaps she could not materialize until she had some energy from the battery.

Other spirits appear in the form of tiny bright orbs and flit about the tree tops. They occasionally wander down to the center of the trees. These feel like young children or possibly sprites (young, fairy-like creatures).

There are tree spirits in at least three locations in the park. Tree spirits are actual spirits of the trees and they have very individual personalities. They are visible to almost everyone who looks for them. Look for natural looking knots and formations that look like faces and watch these to see if they move.

1880s Victorian Ghosts

In November of 2007 I did an investigation of an old 1880 Victorian mansion in Garfield Heights in northeast Kansas City, Missouri with the assistance of Chris Brethwaite and Frank Kithcart. The homeowner, Kent Dicus, reported that he and his friend Michael experienced some unexplainable activity in the home. We took along all of our ghost-hunting equipment for a night-time investigation. Oddly, my digital voice recorder was missing from my bag when I arrived even though I know I put it in just before leaving my house. Thankfully, Chris had his with him. When I returned home that night, the recorder was back in my bag.

When we arrived at the home, I immediately felt a presence of a man in the foyer, however, we proceeded to the kitchen to get our gear ready. We started in the basement, and I felt a heavy, dark feeling. One room in particular had the feeling of death in it, and I picked up a young boy living in that space and having breathing problems. The room was cold, damp and moldy. As we all moved towards the stairs to go back up to the kitchen, we noticed that the string for one of the lights was rotating in a circular fashion like a pendulum even though no one had touched it. It kept going for several minutes, much longer than one would expect.

I was surprised to get results in the first room we went into on the first floor. I heard the word "library" several times and Kent confirmed that that room was indeed originally the library as he had found that word written on the wall behind the fireplace mantel. The EMF meter spiked almost everywhere in the room including areas not around any electrical wiring, and the digital recorder picked up some muffled sounds here.

Next, we moved to the foyer, where I sensed the presence of the original owner of the house. He spoke to me telepathically and said that he designed and built the house and was very proud of it.

Photo taken of the home prior to 1920
Courtesy of Kent Dicus

The house today

He was pleased that the current owners took so much care to restore it to its original condition and use. Over the years it had been used for other purposes, including a home for unwed mothers and later for the elderly. Kent confirmed that the first owner was indeed the designer of the house. The spirit wanted me to go upstairs.

The owners led us to the second floor. The guest room had photographs of ancestors on the mantel. I felt the presence of some particular people that are watching over Kent, and he indicated that he felt that was correct. Then another presence made itself known to me and said she was Michael's Aunt, and she was always with him. These spirits were not the ones responsible for the unusual activity, however, there were still places to investigate.

The team walked down the hall and when someone opened a closed door a small white foggy mist was seen by everyone present. It quickly flew up into the ceiling and disappeared. Upon playback of the video tape in slow motion, the object even leaves a reflection in a mirror in the closet! I felt the presence of two housekeepers in this area, which was close to the servants quarters and stairs. The ghost of the original owner of the house wanted us to go up to the attic and pulled me in that direction.

Not long after walking into the attic area, Michael, Chris, and I all smelled a cherry tobacco pipe burning. There was an area where the owner had built himself a desk/work area and we surmised that this is where he used to escape from the noise of the household to do his work and smoke his pipe. In those days, it was common for the men to have a special area to smoke. Several photos were taken and some of them showed orbs. I felt a lot of activity here, and the homeowner confirmed that they often heard footsteps in the attic and on the attic stairs.

As we passed by the chimney, I was drawn to it and put my

Attic area—note video camera on the right held by an investigator, and several whitish orbs in the photo around the attic ceiling/roof.

Photo taken of the hallway—note small orb on the wall to the right. Other photos of this same area do not show orbs.

hand on it. I could sense carbon monoxide being a health problem for the occupants at some time in the past and that someone became very ill because of this.

Most investigations are not this fruitful. We got high EMF readings in almost every room in the house, most notably in the library, foyer, upstairs bathroom, hall closet and in the attic in places where there were no electronic devices or electric wiring.

Together with the pipe smell, the sounds caught on the digital voice recorder, orbs caught on film, and the fog in the closet, it is my opinion that this house is very haunted, although with quite friendly spirits. The owners wanted to leave the spirits alone since they cause no problems, so we did not ask the ghosts to leave.

Ghost Trains

I saw my first ghost train in 1993 near Wichita, Kansas. My two daughters and I were heading home from a trip when the three of us noticed smoke to the left of the highway. The three of us watched in amazement as an old-fashioned big black steel steam locomotive chugged along, then disappeared into an embankment. We stopped the car to check the area and sure enough, there is a set of railroad tracks that must have been there for some time. They lead directly into the embankment, which must be something that was added later. The train was apparently following its old schedule when we happened to pass by.

We've seen ghost trains in Independence, too. Since our move to Independence in 1987 I noticed a problem with a railroad crossing near my home. It seems to go off of its own accord, even when there is no train in sight. Sometimes the bell continues ringing for a long time, and I have called the railroad on a number of occasions to complain. However, it may not be the fault of the railroad.

While approaching the intersection at Scott and 20th Street one day at approximately 8:00 a.m. I noticed that the red crossing lights were on. I looked down the tracks to the East and saw a train with a small puff of smoke billowing out and its big bright front light on. It appeared to be about a quarter-mile away and moving very slowly. After crossing the track, I looked back but no train was in sight! I realized then that the problems with the crossing probably had nothing to do with the current railroad trains.

This railroad cut and set of tracks dates to the Civil War era, and is the same track that goes by the Lexington house mentioned earlier in this book. I've also noticed a transparent train at the old Independence Depot on a couple of occasions while crossing the bridge on Lexington. The train looks perfectly intact, and is complete with smoke billowing out the top, but you can see through it. The depot is very near the Lexington street location mentioned earlier in this book. I wonder if it is the same train traveling by my house at the Scott intersection? It might be worth a trip to the depot to see if you can see the ghost train.

TIP:

Take photos of nothing—you'll be surprised what comes out when you print the pictures!

Old Ghosts in Fairmount

Fairmount is one of the oldest neighborhoods in Independence. It is located off of 24 Highway. This area was a pioneer village prior to being divided up into Plats in 1860. This particular house was built in 1910 on top of a much older rock foundation and basement. The homeowner's dog digs in the yard and has retrieved farm implements that look very old.

I was first called to investigate this house in 1987 and have returned many times since then. The activity continues to this day. The homeowners, F.K. and his wife A. have experienced spirits materializing on numerous occasions. I have seen one spirit of a man in a long old-west frock coat wearing two pistols. He has long hair and a beard. The man walks up and down the creaking stairs of the house, and can be heard at all times of the day and night. Since the current house was built after the time period of the clothing this ghost wears, I assume that there were steps in the prior house in the same location. This spirit means no harm, and seems unaware of anyone else. He is very serious about his work, and seems to be concentrating hard while he walks. I believe he was a deputy or marshal.

One night shortly after retiring for the evening, A. told. F. to look at their dresser. There, in full Confederate Civil War uniforms and swords were three tiny men standing on the dresser. None of the men were more than 24" high, but all were in perfect proportion. These three ghosts have appeared several times and they do react to the homeowner's when they notice them. A. and F. do not feel any malice from the spirits and do not want them to go. This is my first encounter with ghosts appearing in miniature and I honestly do not have an explanation for it. Obviously, the current house would not have existed during the civil war, but perhaps a camp or cabin was on the property prior to the building of this house.

In May of 2006, F.K. came into possession of his grandfather's white suit from the 1940s. He hung the suit on the outside of the closet and went to bed. A few minutes later, A. saw something in the suit and told F. to look at the suit because his grandfather was standing in it. A. had never seen F's Grandfather, so he asked her to describe him. She did and it was an exact description.

F. could not see his grandfather, but felt his presence, then felt someone lie next to him and put their arm around him. At first, F. thought it was is wife, but when he looked, she was too far away. He sensed that it was no one he knew and this presence had nothing to do with his grandfather, but was a different spirit. F. slowly reached around, grabbed the hand and moved it off of him. F. says the hand was very pliable and felt something like jelly. He was too afraid to turn around to look at what it was. Luckily, he has not experienced it since.

Trance work: I did a scan during a trance and saw a lot of activity over the years. There have been many people living on this spot almost continuously since the 1820s. I saw tents, then a cabin, then saw the cabin being torn down because it was not built very well. Later I saw a foundation being dug and a house built on top of it. That house burned down and was replaced by the current house. At one point, the property was seized (stolen) by someone who kicked out the previous rightful owners.

Historical research: F.K. did some research on at the Historical Society and found that the area was a favorite of Frank James' and that a store he frequented used to be located only 2 blocks from this house. It was a hubbub of activity, so it is no wonder that there are so many spirits here.

5/3/2007: The owners heard the sound of a music box coming from the upstairs bedroom. They do not have a music box. They also heard footsteps walking across the carpeting and stairs for several days in a row. The cat and dog acted strangely during the same time period—often following an unseen object around the room.

05/21/07: Three of the QUEST Team members re-visited the house at the request of the homeowner, who reported recent activity. The team stayed for over three hours, during which time the ghosts were very active. I first sensed something by the fireplace, where I then tested the area with the EMF meter. The meter spiked at the opening of the fireplace.

The three of us felt activity upstairs, so we all moved to the upper floor. As we walked up the steps, our team member Rachel felt a presence in front of her. I should note here that I have seen the spirit of a man on these steps on several occasions. Rachel used the EMF meter, and it spiked, then stopped. As she moved forward, it spiked again. She was able to follow the spirit down the hall and into the far bedroom by using the meter. We had not experienced this before, but this was a very strong spirit. Upon entering the bedroom at the end of the hall, I saw it as it used to be approximately 100 years ago. There was a pot belly stove in the center of the back wall in front of an old chimney, flowered wallpaper on the walls, a simple iron bed, and one dresser. Nothing fancy. The man who lived there was tall and wore a long coat and pistols. I believe this is possibly a deputy marshal or sheriff who rented the room from the owners. I sensed that he reported to work each day in downtown Independence.

Mia, our third team member, then opened the closet door and picked up psychically that someone was once restrained and kept in this room. There was an ominous feeling about it. We all wanted to leave the room immediately. I do not feel this was related to the (possible) marshal.

Trance work: Next we moved to F. and A.'s bedroom. I had the sudden feeling that I should lie down on the bed and close my eyes, and did so. I fell into a half-trance and saw a single mother living in the house with an adult daughter. The daughter and mother were arguing over the daughter going somewhere by herself with no escort. There was no father in the house—I sensed that he was dead. The women both wore long flowered dresses with bustles that could have been late nineteenth century attire. Why this was significant, I don't know yet.

We all moved into the hallway and as I glanced back into the bedroom I saw a column of whitish/green fog appear. I pointed it out to Maria and Rachel and the homeowner, who all saw it, too. It dissipated within a minute. We then looked down the hall to the far bedroom and saw fog again.

F. asked us to look in the bathroom where he saw faces in the carpeting but none of us saw anything there. We then moved downstairs, where a column of fog appeared next to the dining room table. I took a photo (see below) of where the fog appeared, which was to the right and in front of Maria. Maria was just starting to move, so the photo is blurry. But notice her arm—it appears to be transparent. This is exactly where I saw the fog. Note: no one else saw this particular fog except me, however, they did feel the presence of someone nearby.

May 31, 2007: F. reported that he was putting laundry away in his bedroom in the late afternoon when he heard the name "Zizzi" called out by his grandfather's voice. F. had been trying to contact his long-dead grandfather through meditation for some years with no success—until this occurred. He heard no other words. "Zizzi" means "aunt" in Italian, and is what his grandmother's family called her. F. is absolutely certain that it was his grandfather's voice.

June 1, 2007: F. reported to me that as he and his wife had just gone to bed when they both noticed a black, triangular shape object floating in the room. It appeared to be approximately 12" across and was shaped "kind of like the stealth bomber." The object darted about the room, hesitating over several areas, with most of the concentration being over them as they lay in bed. Then the object moved through a closet and into the chimney. The episode lasted approximately 10 minutes.

June 2, 2007: F. reported that a triangular shaped object appeared to them again, only this time it had a greenish glow about it and it stayed for a few minutes longer than the previous evening. This one also moved about the room, then darted through the closet and into the chimney. *Note: See the chapter in this book on haunted chimneys.*

October, 2007: A. told me that she sees ghostly nightgowns and heads of spirits floating in her bedroom at night. F. and A. both saw the full apparition of an old lady in old-fashioned (early 1800s clothing and bonnet) who turned to look at them, then faded away. I decided it was time to find out exactly why there are so many spirits here and asked the couple to leave the house for an hour one evening. As I got comfortable on the couch a black, shapeless shadow moved across the ceiling of the entryway. I knew I was not alone at that point. I meditated and contacted several of the spirits who told me that there is a portal area near the chimney in the bedroom here and that most of them are ex-residents of other houses in the neighborhood.

They use this portal to move in and out of their dimension and sometimes congregate together there. That explains why we see so many non-resident ghosts at this location. They are simply using this spot as a gathering place and to use the portal travel to our dimension. The spirits are not "haunting" the occupants, they just happen to see them as they pass through.

The black shadow does have me a little concerned, though, as it felt rather ominous. Hopefully, it won't return.

July, 2010: The couple continue to have paranormal visitors, especially in the bedroom area. They have also had a number of sightings of what can only be described as tiny UFOs that measure approximately 10" - 12" in diameter. The descriptions are of airplane-like objects, rounded saucer-like objects, and triangular shaped objects both with and without lights. Some even appear to have tiny beings in the windows. Others seem to take photos with flashing lights around the room, then disappear, always in the same location near the chimney.

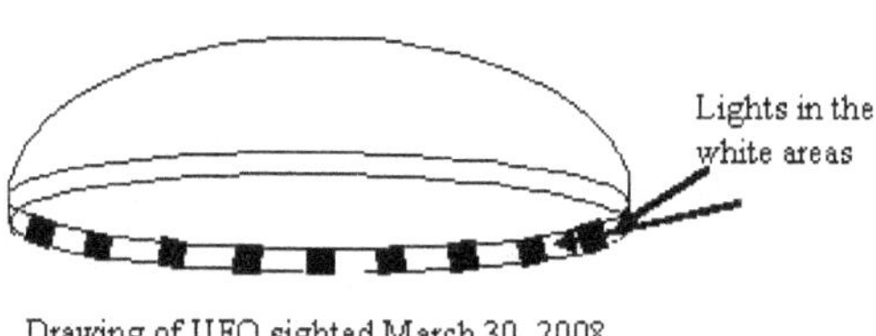

Drawing of one of the tiny UFOs by the homeowner

Pearl House Haunting

This house, built in 1910, was converted to a zone C commercial property and beauty shop in 1970. We purchased it in 2000 and turned it into an office for our staff with the intention of eventually putting up a larger building and tearing down the old house. We moved in and almost immediately knew we were not alone.

The first incident occurred to my secretary. She was missing her scissors, tape dispenser, and stapler. We looked everywhere but could not find them. The next morning they were back in their proper spots. Next, we noticed lights would go off an on of their own accord. And finally, a white mist began to appear to my assistant, then to the rest of us. One day, while she was alone late in the office, my assistant, Tamie, said she saw an old lady walk by her desk and go into my office. The lady was transparent but clearly visible. I began to see the lady not long after. My night bookkeeper reported seeing someone walk through the front office and go into my office on a number of occasions. One evening she took a digital camera and took some photos of my office. In one photo, there is a white mist clearly visible.

We noted that every time we spoke of tearing down the building it angered the spirit and she would react by turning lights off or taking things and hiding them. I have still not retrieved many items and wonder where they are.

We did an investigation of the house and found out that the old woman used to live here by herself for many years and was attached to it. She did not want us to destroy it. During a trance, I also saw other activity from long ago with someone else who owned the property during the 1800s. I see a man wearing a long frock coat and hat who walks around the area surveying it—and I don't see any buildings at all in the area at the time he is looking at it. There are no lingering spirits from that time period, however.

We moved out of the building in 2005 and now use it as a warehouse. I drive by at night sometimes to find all of the lights on even though we know they were turned them off. Note: this house is next door to Pearl House #2 where a ghost likes to turn lights on as well. He might be visiting us at both places.

We have an alarm system and movement sensors on the building. In August of 2006 I was called by our alarm company, Barnhart Security, who said they had movement in the southwest side of the building interior but no open doors or windows. I asked how that was possible and they said they had no explanation since the movement sensor is set at forty pounds. (it takes something at least forty pounds. to set it off). My husband and I rushed to the building and found that a ceiling tile had been moved out of place in the southwest room. The tile was not like that earlier in the day and it is directly below some boxes and items in the attic that we cannot reach. Was the ghost telling us to look at these items? I won't know until we tear the house down.

Haunted Pearl House–Rental

This house is our rental property right next to the office. We purchased it in 2003 to use as a showroom, then turned it into a rental. The first family who rented it stayed for the contract period but left after a year due to ongoing paranormal activity. I saw a man on the roof one evening and thought it was a prankster until he disappeared right in front of my eyes. On at least six other occasions I saw a man looking out of the dining room window, but no one was in the house when we investigated. Other people saw someone looking out of the windows in our direction, too. Lights seemed to go on at night of their own accord, and we all heard footsteps on the basement stairs.

I decided to do an investigation and called the team out one evening. Three of us went into trance and got similar information. During our session we all heard loud footsteps on the basement stairs, but when we went to look there was no one in the area. We searched the whole house but found nothing. We did pick up some muffled voices on the digital audio recorder.

All three of us got information that there was an older man by the name of George who lived in the house alone for many years after his wife died. He got into a routine and did the same thing every day—cooking, getting dressed, reading, turning lights on, etc. He did not like the dark. The man was retired from the military and lived on a fixed income. I did not see a vehicle, so I think he was homebound.

I called my friends at Barnhart Security and told them of the strange events going on. They installed an alarm system for us and then set up an elaborate movement activated camera monitoring system that was hooked up to a computer. The system was in place for two weeks, then the installer took it away to review it. The technician called me and said they were surprised to find something on tape. The T.V. camera was tripped on at 1:00 AM, then the light in the living room came on of its own accord. You could see the switch move up on the video. Now everyone was very excited about this as it proved that something was going on. This was Barnhart's first ghost on tape, and even though no apparition showed up we all felt it was significant and proved that there was an entity in the house. Now Barnhart offers ghost hunting surveillance services.

Subsequently, we have had several QUEST meetings at this house because it is a convenient location for all of us. We have done trance and medium work to work on missing person cases, and have had good results contacting people who have passed on while working at this location. Additionally, during each of our sessions it never fails that some type of paranormal activity will occur. I suspected that there is a ley line or energy vortex at this location, and did dowsing with my L-rods. The rods, say yes, this is a vortex. So it is no wonder we have good luck contacting spirits here.

The 40 Highway Ghost

In late December, 2002, Jamyi McLaughlin took some presents to a friend in Kansas City, Missouri. She was driving in her car alone. Jamyi drove East on 40 Highway from I-70 and when she arrived at 40 Hwy and Manchester saw a 2-car wreck with police and ambulance at the location. The traffic was slow and down to one lane. As Jamyi passed the accident, she noticed that a covered body was being taken out on a stretcher to the ambulance.

She glanced in the rear-view mirror and saw the image of a woman's ghost sitting in the back seat. The apparition had dark brown hair and glazed-over brown eyes. Jamyi was frightened at first, and knew immediately that it was the spirit of the woman from the accident. She decided to ask the woman if she could help her. The woman nodded "yes" stiffly, and when she did so Jamyi noticed that her neck was severely injured.

The woman then spoke out loud and said that she needed to get to her husband to tell him what happened and that "no one knows what happened." She said "Just drive straight ahead." *Note: It is very unusual for a ghost to interact with someone in this manner. I find it very interesting that she could be heard clearly while speaking.*

Jamyi, although still nervous, continued driving straight East on 40. When she got to a trailer park past Sutherland Lumber she saw the woman just step out of the car while the vehicle was moving, apparently headed for the trailer park. A few days later, Jamyi and a friend looked in the obituaries in the newspaper and saw a photo of the same woman who died on the date of the accident. During subsequent visits to the area she has not re-appeared.

Old Independence Library Building and the Lady in Red

228 & 230 W Maple Avenue, Independence, Missouri

This old building on the Independence Square is where two of our stores were once located at Osage and Maple. We moved in during September of 2005 and worked on the stores until January and February until they were opened. We stayed there for three years. The location also housed our offices and our paranormal investigative team met there often to discuss cases. Everyone who spent any amount of time here quickly found out that the place is very haunted.

I found out early on that this structure was built possibly around 1880 on the site of a busy intersection. The building was once the old Independence Library where Bess Wallace worked, and where Harry Truman picked her up every day for lunch before they were married. Harry worked at Clinton's Soda Fountain, which is only two blocks away. The building has also housed a number of businesses in the past including Montgomery Wards. It has been divided in to several shops but the exterior remains the same.

During the period that we worked on the stores to get them ready we did some extensive remodeling. On a number of occasions we had electric power tools stop working even though there was no breaker thrown, then start again. We wondered if a spirit was playing tricks on us. We heard voices on several occasions but when I investigated the source could not find anyone there. The voices continued as long as we occupied the location, often fooling my assistant, our bookkeeper, and Victoria's store manager or one of our clerks into thinking that one of them said something. The voices are usually unintelligible, but on some instances can be clearly heard. Often a disembodied voice will answer a question in a clear "yes" or "no" answer.

Lady in Red: We had a camera set up with a monitor in the back office so we can see when someone enters the store. On several occasions I saw a woman dressed in 1930s clothing. She wears a red skirt, white shirt with red trim on the collar and a red hat. She has short, dark bobbed hair and carries books in her left arm. The lady walks determinedly through the middle of the stores, then through the center of the fireplace store through heavy cast iron stoves we have on display, then through the wall on the East side through a mantel. I believe that wall was an addition to the original building so it may be that it was not there before she died. It seems at times as if she is floating rather than walking, and at other times to walk normally.

More recently, a spirit opens and closes the front doors on each of our stores. The bell goes off and the doors open, but there is no one there. These door are very heavy solid wood and could not possibly open due to wind or any other reason. We have seen some apparitions that look like solid people appear then disappear.

This phenomena occurs almost on a daily basis.
There have been several days when we see someone walk in the store, but when we go to assist them there isn't anyone there. I believe this phenomena is a *Time Imprint,* rather than a haunting. It can occur in places where lots of activity took place over a long period of time, which would certainly be the case here.

October, 2006: We continue to experience spirits on a daily basis. They are especially active during October and November when the veil between the two worlds is thinnest. Sometimes it can get very annoying when you are trying to get your work done and get interrupted by the door bell, go out to greet a customer, and there is no one there - or you hear a person moving around and no one is around the area.

I taught a class on ghost hunting at this location in late October and during the class a couple of the attendees noticed someone walking behind the curtain that leads to my office. No one was in there and there is no other way out. They were quite excited to have seen a ghost appear during the class.

After the class, I was talking to Chris Brethwaite, a friend of mine who is a paranormal researcher. Chris was drawn to an area in front of a mantel display where he saw a woman appear. I did not see her, but felt a presence and saw a white mist. I walked to the area and we both noticed a very cold spot at that location. I took an EMF reading, and the meter spiked in that area. The spot warmed up after about 2 minutes.

December, 2006: A heavy Sony camera and case flew off of one of our bookshelves while we had a lot of customers in both stores. I heard rustling of papers before it happened but was too busy to investigate. I got the feeling that the spirit was upset that we weren't paying attention to it. I asked it to quit the pranks and they stopped for a few days.

January, 2007: My assistant and I were talking over lunch one day and I told her about how my deceased grandfather, Boyd Kithcart, recently contacted me while I was trying to communicate with my other grandfather, Frank Lombardo. Right as I explained how he contacted me we both heard a violent shaking of metal objects next to the window in the office. I looked around the area and found no metal except for a heavy file cabinet. I don't know how that sound was made, but we both figured that Boyd was just letting us know that he is alive (in spirit) and well.

June 4, 2007: I was watching the monitor when I saw a man's head appear in the store, then turn and go through a wall. The head was completely black. This is something new.

July, 2007: We had another alarm go off at the store –
this is the fourth time it has been set off for no apparent reason. The alarm company said movement is setting it off, but we can find nothing in the stores that could move- except for ghosts. Two police officers met me at the store to examine the area. I finally told them after talking with them for 15 minutes that the only thing I could figure was ghostly activity, and to my surprise, they were not surprised at all. The officers told me that they get frequent paranormal calls in Independence. Now, I know there is a lot of haunting going on in this town, but for it to be so widespread that the police think nothing of it is amazing.

October, 2007: I taught the "Haunted Independence" class here one evening and we had three incidents. Several people told me they saw the heavy curtains I have in a doorway move on their own. These are too heavy to move due to air currents from the air conditioning. It is the same location where someone saw an apparition during class last year. I saw the floating head of a man appear in front of one wall, and another woman saw it, too. She described it exactly as I saw it—with dark circles around his eyes and very creepy looking.

Next, a woman in the class said she saw a lady wearing a white lace dress that was calf-length and black patent leather shoes. The lady kept saying "look at me—I'm very fashionable." She has blond hair. This is the exact same description that Chris Brethwaite gave me the previous year of a ghost that appeared to him in the same location. We felt her presence at the front of the store.

This is an example of how spirits may appear when you talk about them, and it is fairly common. I guess it would be curiosity on their part—or maybe they are just letting us know that "yes, we are here."

Haunted Chimneys

Are chimneys portals to other dimensions? Do spirits enter and return through these portals? Since my contracting company does chimney inspections and repair, we are around fireplaces and chimneys constantly. We have noticed a pattern of ghostly activity and orbs around chimneys, and I am beginning to think that this sort of activity is fairly common. I also have a theory as to why paranormal events happen around chimneys, but more about that later.

I have thousands of pictures of chimneys and fireplaces taken with digital cameras. We started noticing that orbs were showing up in some pictures when a very dramatic photo with colored orbs showed up in May of 2003 (see chapter 7– Photographing Ghosts). This was the first time I noticed anything unusual in the photos, and it prompted me to watch for other anomalies around chimneys when inspection reports come in. We started using digital cameras in 1999, before that we used 35 mm film which never showed anything out of the ordinary.

Digital cameras pick up more of the Ultra Violet spectrum, so they sometimes get things that the naked eye can't see. In all but one case, the inspector did not see anything at the time, but the strange items appeared when the disk was put in the computer.

In the past several years we have collected quite a few photos that show something unusual in them such as colored orbs, white orbs, white streams of heavy fog, and in one instance—a clearly defined face of a man in the back fireplace wall. In every case, I compared the rest of the photographs taken at the same time and of the same chimney, and in all but one instance they show nothing unusual. It is usually *one* photograph that catches something, and the rest of the photos at the same location don't show anything. There is only one chimney so far where an orb appeared three different photos from different angles, and in the case of the face in the fireplace, it can still be seen with the naked eye at the home.

We do approximately five inspections per day with 6-12 photos taken at each house, so the photos with anomalies are only a small fraction of the total number of photos we have on file. In my opinion, that means that it is probably pretty rare to catch an orb or ghost on film.

Ghostly Encounters Around Chimneys

In 1989 our company swept 350 chimneys at Fort Leavenworth, Kansas. We ran into three ghosts at Leavenworth that were rather uncooperative and apparently did not appreciate us disturbing them. The fort was established in 1827, and has a long history of spirits. At least nine ghosts have been officially reported, but there are likely more that have not been reported. During our work, several highly unusual events occurred that can only be attributed to the paranormal. Unfortunately, we do not have photos of any fireplaces since photography is not allowed on the base. All of the chimneys are constructed with bricks and mortar.

House #1: This house is the oldest building on the post and was originally a chapel. The chapel burned down in approximately 1827, and a clergyman named Father Fred was killed in the fire. A new house was built on the same spot in the 1830s— presumably using the same chimney. While we were sweeping the chimney, coal dust started coming through the entire masonry wall in the living room. There were no holes or cracks in the masonry! The entire lower level of the house was dusted with fine, grey coal soot and we had to go back and spend 8 hours vacuuming and cleaning up. What a mess! I was mortified, since nothing like that had ever happened to us.

The colonel's wife was not upset at all, and calmly explained to me that the problem must have been caused by their resident ghost! She told me that right after moving in to the house, they hosted a party for the officers and their wives. During the party, a woman screamed when she saw a face of a man in the fire in the fireplace. Everyone in attendance saw the same thing and ran screaming out of the house. Evidently, it was quite a scene. After that, the family saw the apparition of a man floating on the landing next to the chimney on several occasions. He was wearing a clergy outfit, but his feet did not materialize when he appeared. He also appeared on many occasions in the fire, so the family quit using the fireplace. Well, at least it is clean now. I hope that ghost appreciates it.

House #2: Built in the later 1800s, this is a large three-story home. The occupant (the wife of an officer) notified us upon arrival that the room we were going to be working in was haunted, and the ghost often closed the door. She noted that she was leaving the door open all the way and that the door was off balance leaning in towards the room, then she left us to our work. I tarped off the fireplace, then sent a tech up to the top of the chimney to start sweeping. While standing alone in the room, the door suddenly slammed shut. I quickly ran over to the door and opened it to see if anyone was around, but there was no one in the hall. I then heard strange noises and talking coming from the fireplace and called the sweep on the radio to see what was going on. She said she did not

Photos courtesy of HearthMasters, Inc.

I have found in my own investigations and have heard from other ghost hunters that spirits often appear in or around fireplaces and chimneys. My theory is that the draft created by the chimney creates a portal between dimensions.

Diagram of a typical masonry chimney

I suspect that ghosts use chimneys to travel to and from the spirit world and they do so through draft.

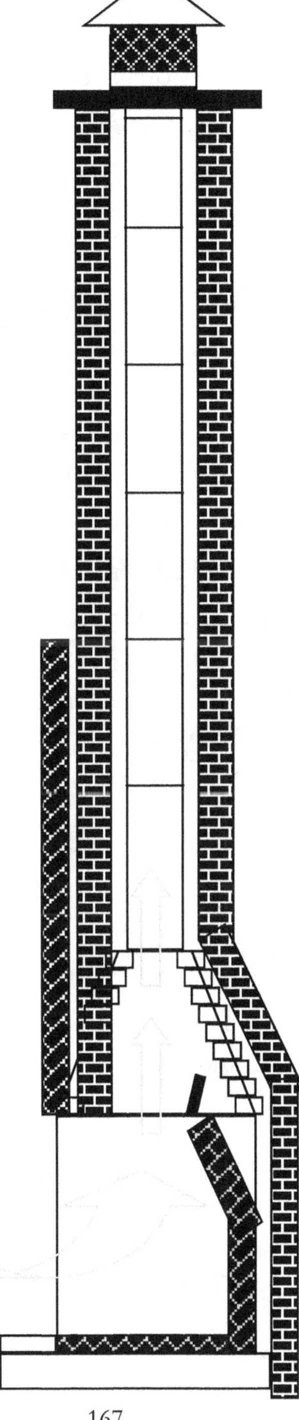

Draft can reverse when something is not working right or if the house is under negative pressure.

say anything, and of course there was no one else on the chimney with her. When the lady of the house returned, she was not surprised to hear about the goings–on. She also told me that it was common knowledge among the residents at Fort Leavenworth that there is a lot of ghostly activity going on in the older houses. We packed up our gear and got out as quickly as we could.

House #3: Built around 1840, this is a two-story brick house with slate roof and brick chimney. I was outside by the van talking to the homeowner. One tech was inside at the fireplace, and another tech was outside on top of the roof doing the sweeping. Suddenly the 40' ladder fell over on it's side—seemingly pushed by someone who wasn't there. The occupant and I both saw it fall over. The sweep walked over to the place where the ladder was but could not get down until we got the ladder back up again. This was a 40' heavy aluminum ladder that weighs 80 lbs.! There was no wind that day *and* it was tied down to the gutter with a bungee cord! I had to call in another crew to get the ladder back up so the sweep could get down. The occupant of the home told me that they have a mischievous ghost who lives with them and causes havoc frequently. He said that the ghost hung around the fireplace most of the time.

I did an internet search to see if there was any more information about Fort Leavenworth, and it turns out there are several books written about the subject that you can buy at the museum on the post, and other information on websites. From *hauntedhouses.com* I found the following information regarding the fireplace at 605 McClellan, located in the McClellan Officer's quarters. This house is a large three-story home. Apparently when a family moved in this house in 1975, a spirit made itself known to them. While enjoying a warm fire in the fireplace, the family was "gripped with fearful fascination" when an apparition of a man with a mustache and goatee appeared in the middle of the flame. When the fire died out, the face of this ghostly man appeared and remained on the back of the fireplace. This case sounds like the face in the fireplace I mentioned earlier.

Recently a program on ghosts was presented on the Discovery Channel. The occupants of the house said that every psychic investigator that has gone through the home notices that one of the entities comes in through the flue and stands in front of the fireplace. The temperature where the ghost stands is noticeably colder than the surrounding area. Other TV programs and internet articles mention ghosts around chimneys.

Why Chimneys Attract Spirits

In doing research on ghosts in the Kansas City area I talked with several other ghost hunters including Chris Brethwaite, a local Kansas City paranormal investigator and author. Chris and others have mentioned to me that they have noticed more paranormal activity around rivers, streams, and railroad tracks. I realized that in our ghost hunts that was true. A graveyard next to a river is more active than one that isn't. I got to thinking about what those features have in common with chimneys. It is *movement.* There is a flow of energy in any river, stream, or railroad track. And the correlation with chimneys is *draft*, the only difference being that chimneys are vertical rather than horizontal.

All chimneys are designed to create draft to remove toxic flue gasses and smoke from the fireplace or appliance without mechanical means. It is simply physics that makes a chimney work. The temperature differential between the outside of the chimney and the inside of the house is basically what creates draft. Draft is different at certain times of the year, being stronger in the cold winter months, which is also the time of year that people spend more time around the fireplace and fire up their gas furnace. However, draft in a chimney occurs all of the time, even when it reverses because something is wrong with the system or house. The pictures we have taken of orbs are from all seasons of the year.

The Most Haunted House in Missouri?

Note: Do not try to visit—this is a private residence

I could write an entire book on this extremely haunted house. My family moved into this large 1850s home on Calhoun Street in Springfield, Missouri near Drury College in 1972. The first time I walked over the threshold I passed through a cold spot and said to my mother "This place is haunted." I was 14 at the time. She felt the cold spot, too, and agreed with me.

The night we moved in this Civil-war era home we had all just gone to bed when we heard my sister, who had a room at the end of the hall, scream. My father and 9-year old brother and I ran to find out what was wrong. I looked at the bed and spoke to her. In the dark you could see someone in the bed with the covers on, and we thought it was my sister. However, her voice then came from the closet where my sister was hiding and she said there was a ghost in her bed. I turned the light on and as I did so, we all saw a ghost of a man in the bed who promptly disappeared -and we watched the covers slowly fall down. After that my sister moved her bed into the closet. The ghostly visits were a daily occurrence.

Not long after settling in the house I noticed something odd about the walls. I could see small 3" -5" size three-dimensional faces of people in the walls. The faces moved around and talked, but I could hear no sound. At first, I was a little frightened but saw that they were oblivious to me, and I was just watching scenes from the past (time imprints). There were so many different faces that I wondered where these people could possibly have come from. We decided to investigate the past history of the place and found out that a doctor used the house as a hospital. That was the reason for the elevator, and it would explain the presence of spirits and the number of faces in the walls. In later years, my mother admitted to seeing the faces, too, but she didn't tell me at the time because she didn't want me to be afraid.

We often heard footsteps walking on the wood floors and the cat would follow invisible things around the rooms. Sometimes the cat would jump in our laps as if she were afraid of something unseen.

One day, I was home alone doing ironing and listening to James Brown on the radio when an announcement came on that a man just escaped from the local jail. A few minutes later I heard loud footsteps on the stairs and second floor. I thought my father had come home and entered through the back door as usual, then went upstairs. However, when I looked out the back door his car was not there.

I had no way to contact my mother so I called the police, who thoroughly checked out the entire house. They asked me if I knew there was a shotgun on my parent's bed, and I said I had no idea if my dad had it out or not, but that he did own a gun. The police left and I locked up the house. Later, when my family returned I found out that no one had taken the shotgun out of the locked cabinet. They caught the jail inmate shortly later on the other side of town.

So apparently,

this ghost could not only make loud stomping noises, but also had the ability to get a gun out of a locked gun safe! Sometime during the summer I had a chilling event happen at around 9:30 pm. I had just gone to bed when I noticed a very white/blue light shine through my window. It was so bright it almost blinded me. I could not locate the source of the light, but something caught my attention in the vanity mirror across the room. I clearly saw a woman dressed in a black high-necked old-fashioned 1900s dress with a wide-brimmed hat. She was stabbing a younger woman who was wearing a white dress with a large knife. The young woman was screaming, but I could hear nothing It was as if I was looking at a reflection of something in the mirror that happened at this location sometime in the past.

To add to the drama, the large Victorian mansion just two doors down from us has its own story, which may or may not be related to the goings on at this house. We looked up newspaper archives and found out that a famous dentist lived and worked in the mansion in the late 1900s. He was obsessed with teeth, and kept all that he pulled. Apparently, this doctor went insane and when Mayor's wife visited him to have one tooth pulled, she woke up to find all of her teeth gone!

This incident so enraged the Mayor that the dentist knew he was headed for jail, so instead he took his own life by hanging himself in the house. The story leaked to the press and apparently the dentist's son could not take the bad attention and killed himself in the same manner. I wonder if the energy in this area is so bad that it affects the houses around it, including the one I lived in.

In 2004 while in Springfield for a convention, my friend Donna and I stopped by the house. I wanted to see if it was still

The bedroom window where the bright light and vision of a murder appeared

Back of house from alley. Top window on the right is where the ghost appeared in my sister's room.

haunted after over 30 years, and she agreed to accompany me to the front door. My intention was to talk to the current owner, but I noticed that there were no shades on the windows and only a few books strewn on the floor. It looked vacant, but I rang the doorbell anyway.

The house is arranged so that you can see inside the window of the front door, through the window of the foyer door, and out through the window of the back door. The sun was shining through the back door and illuminated everything inside. Donna and I were about to leave when I decided to try the bell again. She and I both saw an old woman with white hair dressed in a long black dress walk slowly around the corner in front of the back door. She was using a cane. Then the woman disappeared before our eyes. Donna immediately turned and left saying "*Looks like it's still haunted and I'm not hanging around for more*!"

I could see several people inside one tiny cell because there was no room for all of the inmates. Some of the people had done nothing wrong and felt greatly wronged by their accusers. I heard crying that sounded like children or young women, and saw a pregnant woman. Later I found out that women and children who were "on the wrong side" were kept in the jail just before and during the Civil War.

Upon entering Frank James' cell I immediately felt his presence and personality. Knowing nothing of Frank prior to this visit, I was surprised to find that he was intelligent, could read and write quite well, and was obviously well–educated and well-mannered. Surprisingly, I did not sense that he was really a bad guy, or that he thought he was bad at all, which was not exactly what I was expecting from an outlaw. When we toured the museum later I found that my assessment of Frank was exactly right, and that he was friends with the governor of Missouri and other high officials.

While still in Frank's cell I picked up another, more sinister spirit. This was a lingering ghost who stays behind and lives in that cell or near it. The spirit is a tall heavy-set Caucasian man with dark long hair that he pulls back. He also wears a long beard. He feels that he is trapped in this location forever and he is somewhat insane. I believe that he takes energy from people who visit and that keeps his spirit going. I would not attempt to confront him as he is extremely negative.

I then saw a tall African-American man incarcerated here who has a strong personality, was a murderer, and was afraid of no one in his lifetime. I also saw a fight between two prisoners who were in cells across from each other. Interestingly, a lady and her daughter came into my shop recently and related a story about how during their visit to the jail someone grabbed the daughter's arm and when she looked around there was no one there. Then she saw two men in Civil war uniforms (one Union, one Confederate) fighting and shaking their fists at each other through the cell bars. One man was released from his cell and the guard handed him his guns. The man then turned and shot and killed the man he was arguing with right in front of the guard. The woman was so frightened by this sight that she will not return for another visit.

We toured the Marshal's home and when we got to the large bedroom area upstairs I could feel the presence of a strong woman. She does not want to leave and is very attached to the home. She feels that it is her home and all the visitors that go through there now are intruders. The woman does walk around to other parts of the building, including the gift shop area, and lets people know she is there. I hear the name of Cassie.

Note: every year during October, the Independence Square Association hosts ghost tours, and the jail is one of the stops. Go to www.theindependencesquare.com for more information.

Thurnham Hall, Lancaster, England

My husband and I made a trip to England in April of 2005 and stayed in a wonderful 12th century Jacobean stone manor house called *Thurnham Hall.* Immediately upon entering the hall I felt the presence of several spirits. One was a short, very stocky man with red hair who was trying to get his big leather lace-up boots off. I had visions of straw on the floor and animals inside the building. The man took off a sword that looked to big for him to carry. I asked where he was from and he said in a heavy accent "Scotland, of course." He came here on an invitation from the king and was helping to fight and protect the lands. This was a very early time period— the 1100s— and he was still very attached to the place. The ghost often pulled tricks on guests because he felt that he still had some ownership of the place, but he was very much aware that he was dead.

The second spirit was that of an older woman whose domain was the kitchen and lower level. She told me she was the head of the household and was in charge of the manor. I saw a little boy near her who was very attached to her. This child's parents were not around much and the older woman took care of him most of the time.

On the third evening of our stay, the activities director took the guests on a tour of the building and told stories of the ghosts that choose to occupy several rooms in the large hall. I couldn't wait to hear what he had to say, since I already knew this place had several spirits. He told us of several reports by guests of children in old-fashioned clothing playing on the grounds, and a ghostly woman who picks up twigs on the lawn.

Our guide then showed a VCR tape of a room that had been occupied by a man who killed his wife in the 1700s. The tape had been made by a film crew from British television who brought along a psychic to do research for a program on ghosts. I filmed the TV screen as the guide played the tape for us.

Everyone in the room gasped as hundreds of tiny white glowing orbs appeared. The orbs came to the top of the fireplace opening, hesitated a second, then quickly exited the fireplace into the room. Most shot across the room and through the walls in several different directions. This continued for at least two full minutes. I checked the chimney for draft after everyone left the room and it was drafting strongly UP, so any theory about dust particles mistaken for orbs coming DOWN the chimney can be ruled out.

Next, the tour guide took us to the library where we all sat around in chairs while he and his wife stood on the balcony and explained that Jane Seymour lived in the hall before her (unfortunate) betrothal to King Henry VIII. The guide also said that the ghost of an old woman had been spotted in the library and the chapel next to it. Just before he started talking about the ghost, I saw an apparition of an elderly lady wearing floor-length skirts walk right through the guide's wife and head towards the chairs on the balcony. No one else in the room saw this, so I kept quiet, all the while thinking that the current tenants really have no idea how haunted Thurnham Hall is.

The Ghost Children

I worked on a missing person case a few years ago involving two children who were kidnapped by their father. The case was highly publicized, but I didn't know about it until one day six months after their disappearance when I saw their pictures at the local grocery store. I immediately knew that I was connected to these children somehow. I'd never had that feeling with other missing person notices, or with missing person cases I worked on. I immediately got in contact with the children's mother and my daughter and I met with her and her sister.

At our first meeting I went into a light trance and heard the children's father talking to a number of people including his sister, mother, brother, neighbors, and friends. Each time he discussed a different set of plans regarding what he was planning to do with the children after the kidnapping, so it was extremely confusing as to what actually happened.

Naturally, the mother was anxious to know where her children were and what happened to them. Even though the father sat in jail with the threat of a prison sentence, he would not tell police what happened. His story changed daily. I even tried to "read" him from a distance, but was not successful in discovering what he had done, likely because he had all kinds of scenarios in his head.

Not long after our first meeting, both of my daughters and I started having psychic communication with the two children. We got extremely detailed locations and conversations with the people involved. The children told me they were alive and could be located near a bend in a large river and other body of water below ground level, near railroad tracks and an unnamed street. I thought that this meant they were alive and held in some sort of bunker under the ground. When I told their mother this she said it would not be inconceivable because their father was a skilled survivalist and could have built something like that easily.

One of the children spoke to me and said that she was near an unnamed street, a railroad track, near a bend in a river, and another body of water nearby. I dowsed a map with a pendulum and was pulled to two locations: Arkansas near a river with a bend in it, and the Missouri River near Hannibal, Missouri. The Arkansas location had railroad tracks and an unnamed street, and was near where the father's mother lived. We thought this must be the location. The little girl was in contact with me telepathically on and off for months, but never indicated that they were in any trouble. I then contacted a detective who was working on this case but he never called me back.

A fourth member of our investigative team then went to a particular park because she was 'pulled' to go there. She heard children's voices as if they were playing, but could not locate any children. She didn't think anything about it at the time and did not tell us about it, she just thought they must be ghost children and didn't make any connection to this case. Then one day in January, I had the sudden urge to visit that same park. My daughters and I had never been there, but I was again told by one of the children's voices to go to that location. My oldest daughter called me that same day and said she wanted to go visit that park. She'd had a dream that the little girl was playing in a park with many other children, however they were all in spirit form. She'd drawn a picture of the parking area, a tree, and a sidewalk that were very vivid in her dream. Now I was convinced that something was going on.

I went into trance, and the little girl told me she was there with her brother. So the three of us went to the location. I happened to drive to the exact spot where our fourth team member heard children's voices months before. My daughter stopped and became dizzy with shock. This area matched her dream and drawing in exact detail. She was overwhelmed. We all got out and were drawn to a particular spot near the woods and felt strongly that we were on to something. I felt strong pull to a location deeper in the woods and wanted to go back and get some shovels and dig where I was being pulled. However, we knew this was not a good idea.

The missing little girl visited me in my dreams often, showing me where she and her brother were and what they were doing. There were many places they visited, even relatives homes in other states. The entire time I thought she was alive because the images were so vivid. I had worked on many missing persons cases before this, all were adults, and all were deceased and knew it. The only other case involving a young child turned out good because she was found alive at the address I found, but the child did not communicate telepathically, I was just able to find her vibration. So I had no experience with deceased children up to this point.

Several months later, I went in to a trance to work on another case when the same little girl popped in and spoke to me. She said they could see the fireworks from where they were on the July 4 on the Missouri River. The next morning I heard banging on my bathroom wall that was so hard it moved the picture on the wall. The picture is a boat on a river. I shared this information with my team and we met to talk about it. We thought: boat = river. So we got out a map and sure enough, there is the bend in the Missouri river, the water works was near it, as were railroad tracks and an unnamed street. All too coincidental.

I did another trance session and spoke with the little girl. This time she showed me what happened. Their father had taken them out to the woods and shot them both and buried them in the ground. He told them that they would all (including their mother) soon be together and that this was the only way.

The little girl had just come to realize, partly because of our telepathic communication over the months, that she and her brother had passed over and were in spirit form. She said they were both doing okay, but that she felt the need to get this resolved for her family's sake, and so that she and her brother could move on to other things as they were supposed to do. She said they felt alive, and did not know they had actually left their bodies until recently. I contacted their mother, but did not tell her what I knew. I asked her to have the FBI contact me so I could tell them some things, but no one called me back. I asked her to do this a second time, but still no one called me back. I was ready to talk to the FBI or police because we were so certain of our findings. Two days after this second request, the children were found in the exact location that we knew they were.

This case was frustrating and very sad, but it taught me a lesson: people, especially children, may not know they have died for some time, and may need help seeing that and moving on. Some ghosts really don't realize they have died because they feel so alive. It also demonstrates that the spirit world can give you detailed information that can be very useful in solving mysteries.

A Ghost Extraction

Sometimes ghosts will appear in the least likely places. Claudia Green and George Miles from Kansas City asked me to assist them in getting a ghost to leave them alone.

The week before contacting me the ghost of their friend had appeared in the rear-view mirror of their car—apparently sitting in the back seat- as they were passing by the spot where the friend had died in a car accident exactly one year before. It was the anniversary of their friend's death. The ghost of their friend appeared to them as a full body apparition, and had been sitting on their beds leaving an indentation in the covers, speaking out loud, and physically touching their arms.

After I contacted the spirit of their deceased friend during a trance session, I asked her to tell me something that only her friends would know as confirmation that I was indeed speaking to the correct person. She told me to tell her friends that she always wore blue eye shadow, and they confirmed that it was indeed the correct spirit since their friend was known for her blue eye shadow.

It turned out that the spirit was just trying to give the two friends comfort, and was still on the earth plane because Claudia and George kept saying things like " I wish she wasn't gone," and "I wish she were here," Naturally, the ghost of their friend was just doing as they asked, and was trying to comfort them, not scare them.

I asked the friends if they were ready to let her go, and they said yes. I told the spirit of their friend to go with her spirit guides to the light. She did and has not returned since.

Bullock Hotel. Photo by Margie Kay

The Bullock Hotel

Deadwood, South Dakota is one of the most haunted towns I've ever had the fortune to visit. As an avid ghost hunter for over 38 years, I thought I'd seen almost everything, but Deadwood is the exception to the rule.

Besides being known for its rich history of outlaws, murderers, gold seekers, and of course, the site where Wild Bill Hickok was murdered, Deadwood has the unique distinction of being the only entire town on the National Historic Register.

When Deadwood was first founded it was in direct violation of a treaty with the Lakota people. The Lakotas had legal land ownership, however, when Colonel George Armstrong Custer led an expedition into the Black Hills in 1874 and discovered gold there, a gold rush began that gave rise to the town of Deadwood, which quickly rose to a population of 5,000 in town and over 15,000 prospectors in the area. The gold seekers and fortune hunters were living on the land illegally, but that didn't stop them. The prospect of finding gold was just too big to pass up. One local gold mine just closed as recently as 2001, and the word from the locals is that there is still a lot of gold to be found in the area, but most if it is in bedrock.

The town soon grew with businesses, both legitimate and illegitimate. The business of prostitution brought in a lot of money, and was legal until 1980. An entire city block was occupied by nothing but brothels at one point, run by such infamous Madams as Mustache, Pam, and Dirty Em, as did gambling and sales of opium. The lawless town had no sheriff until Seth Bullock, owner of the Bullock Hotel and other businesses, took the job not long after Hickok was murdered by Jack McCall in 1876.

After the gold rush slowed, the area soon began mining for other ores, which kept the economy thriving. In 1876 a smallpox epidemic swept through the town, killing many. Other epidemics killed many children and adults, who are now buried in mass graves.

Some of the towns most famous residents and visitors included Al Swearengen, owner of the Gem Theatre; Sol Star, partner of Seth Bullock; Potato Creek Johnny, famous for finding a gold nugget the size of a potato; and Calamity Jane, friend of Wild Bill Hickok.

Some Interesting Facts about Deadwood:

• Kevin Costner owns a casino in Deadwood called *The Midnight Star,* so named from the movie *Silverado.*

• Prostitution wasn't outlawed in Deadwood in 1980.

• The town once was home to over 5,000 people, but now hosts only 1,300 residents (not counting tourists).

• Deadwood's popularity increased greatly due to the popular HBO series "Deadwood," resulting in a huge increase in tourism in the spring and summer months.

• Snow accumulation can reach 60 inches, but city-owned snow removal trucks take care of it quickly.

• The Bullock Hotel was the subject of the TV show *Unsolved Mysteries.*

We stayed at the Bullock Hotel, built by entrepreneurs Seth Bullock and Sol Star in 1894-96. Seth and Sol were partners in a hardware store that they moved to Deadwood from Helena, Montana. Bullock had been sheriff in Lewis and Clark County, Montana before his arrival in Deadwood. Bullock's grandson described him as "Tall, with steely gray eyes and an imposing appearance that commanded respect. It was said that he could outstare a mad cobra or a rogue elephant."

This beautiful hotel at the corner of Main and Wall streets was built with native pink and white sandstone. It has been restored to its Italianate Victorian style. This is the oldest hotel in Deadwood.

We stayed in the Roosevelt Suite on the second floor where many strange events have occurred. It seems that Seth Bullock or "Old Seth," as the employees call him, haunts the second floor where he

is said to have died in room 211 in 1919, and the third floor, as well as the basement bar area and the bar off the lobby. I hoped to have some ghostly encounters and I was not disappointed.

Right after our arrival and before doing any interviews, we decided to take a quick nap, and while my husband was in the shower I lay down on the bed. A few minutes later, a man's voice said my name— "Margie," very loudly. I opened my eyes and looked around but saw no one. My husband said he did not call me. Later that evening, while interviewing employees, I found out that "Old Seth" likes to call out women's names, but that he usually does this for employees and rarely for guests. Since we had just arrived Seth must have been paying attention and followed us to our room immediately after our arrival. Later, the entire king size bed was shoved very strongly by something right after I got in it.

The Bullock did not have its regularly scheduled ghost tour available but one of the staff members was kind enough to take us on a tour of Bully's Bar in the basement, so named for Bullock's lifelong friend, Teddy Roosevelt. The history of the basement is that the existing hotel was built on the older stone foundation. There is an underground stream running right next to a wall, and sometimes when it rains a lot it leaks, which it did for us.

Apparently during the smallpox epidemic there was no place to quarantine people so Bullock allowed sick people to be quarantined in the basement of the original building. Guests and employees sometimes see the apparition of a little girl wearing late 1800s attire in the basement area, and they assume she was a victim of the epidemic of 1876.

The hotel, which was known as a luxury establishment for gentlemen and ladies, used to have a secret underground passageway in the basement which led to a house of prostitution across the street. At the time, it was inappropriate for gentlemen to be seen entering such an establishment, so this way they could go unnoticed by the general public. Gene and I both sensed the presence of spirits there, and took several photographs, but none materialized for us in that location.

We then interviewed several more of the employees and several guests who overheard our conversations. Each of them had a story or two to tell:

- A guest said she kept hearing her name being called and could smell cigar smoke in her room. The entire hotel is non-smoking.
- A front desk clerk said that a photo of Seth kept falling off the wall in the office and they finally had to move it to another location.

- An employee was working in the slot machine cage when a maintenance worker asked for some keys. She had the keys on her finger, when they suddenly levitated slowly out to a distance of 12" and dropped behind a cash drawer.
- A bartender often hears noises or witnesses glasses or full bottles of liquor fly across the room of their own accord. Once a glass fell off of a shelf and hit her on the head. The glasses are normally placed back from the edge of the shelf. The bartender said that paranormal things happen if an employee stops working or takes a break. They often feel a hand on their shoulder, or hear their name spoken. It seems that Mr. Bullock is making sure that "his" employees are not slacking off!
- A guest complained to the front desk that his room 211 suddenly filled with cigar smoke. He assured the staff that he was not a smoker and he didn't want to be accused of smoking in the room.
- A guest told me that when she stayed in room 313 her 10-year-old put his toy stuffed wolf down in the bedroom, but when he turned around to pick it up again, it had been moved into the shower of its own accord.
- A couple of the employees have heard strange unexplained children's voices over the phone intercom system, but can't find a reason for the sounds.

After hearing these tales, I continued my own ghost hunt. The bar on the first level was now closed, so I asked permission to enter and take photos with my Sony night vision still camera while my husband listened to more ghost stories from the maintenance worker. I snapped a few pictures, then felt a presence to my right at the bar.

I raised the camera and just as I did so saw two bright white orbs of light floating behind the bar, and moving towards and through the wall. These were not visible to the naked eye, but could clearly be seen through the large LCD viewfinder of the camera. One orb was in front of the other, and slight trails showed up in the viewfinder. I was not fast enough in snapping the photo to get these orbs on film, however. Darn!

I then focused my attention upstairs. It was 1:00 a.m. and my husband went to sleep. I quietly entered the hallway on the second floor to take some pictures and video when a woman came down the stairway from the third floor. She accused me of talking with someone else loudly outside her bedroom door on the third floor and waking her up. I had heard nothing, and certainly was not on the third floor or making any noise myself. In fact, I had just gone into the hall when she came out of her door. What she heard may have been ghostly voices.

A few photos I took with my still camera had anomalous items in them. What looks like a wishbone shape appears in the second

Unexplained foggy shape in the Bullock Hotel taken by a guest.
Courtesy of the Bullock Hotel

Photo of the second floor mirror at the Bullock taken with my night-vision camera.
Notice the wishbone shape in the mirror.

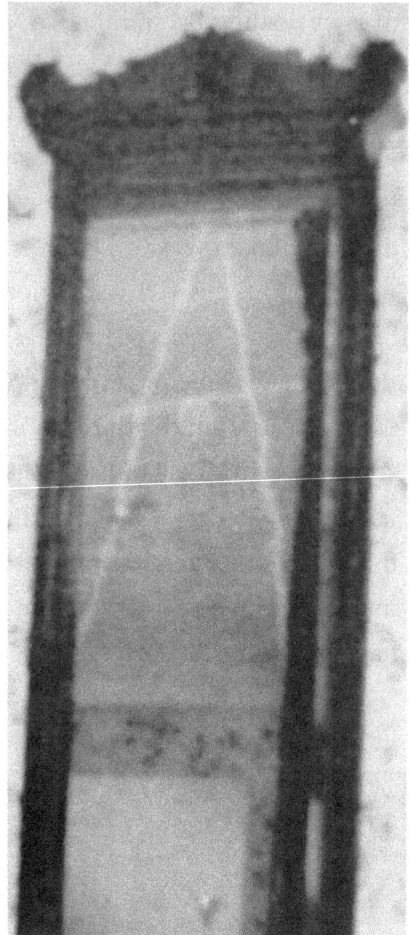

Photo taken by a guest—shows an "A" in the mirror. (Courtesy of the Bullock Hotel)

floor hallway mirror where many other people have often captured a similarly shaped letter "A," I was able to capture two more anomalous shapes on the wall in the downstairs bar. The shape changes slightly between two photos taken in the bar.

A search through a large book near the front desk containing photos and letters from hotel guests reveal that the haunting has been going on for many years.

The **Mount Moriah Cemetery**, which sits atop a big hill looking over Deadwood, is the final resting place of many of Deadwood's citizens. The first location of the cemetery, called Ingleside Cemetery, was in the same city block as the famed Adams House Museum, but was later moved to the hill after a severe flood washed many of the graves and coffins away. Tour guides mentioned that some coffins were actually taken right to the middle of Main Street during the 1882 deluge. During renovations, many homeowners have found skeletal remains in the area over the years.

Will Bill Hickok, Calamity Jane, Potato Creek Johnny, Seth Bullock, and many others are buried at Mount Moriah. Caretakers report that sightings of shadowy ghosts and unexplained voices have been reported by visitors. After closing time, caretakers have sometimes heard people talking in the locked cemetery, but when they investigate no one is to be found. I felt like I was being watched by unseen eyes during my 2006 visit and again in 2011.

The **Oyster Bay Restaurant,** at 626 Main Street, is part of the *Fairmont Hotel and Oyster Bay Casino.* The ***Oyster Bay Saloon*** has been at the same location since 1877 when the original owner brought oysters in on ice from the Mississippi river. It seems that the spirit haunting this site is not so benevolent.

The bartender told us that he has had fully secured glasses fall on his head several times. An ex-employee named Sabrina, said that she was filling up napkin dispensers one evening after closing when all nine dispensers came flying at her, cutting one of her arms. She also said that part of the hotel was once made into apartments on the third floor, but that people moved out after being attacked in their rooms by unseen forces. It is believed that those apartments are now closed and unused.

Another employee was closing up one evening after hours and saw a cowboy sitting at one of the slot machines. She started to walk towards him to tell him they were closed, but he "just disappeared into thin air."

Our next stop was the **Gem Theatre**, site of one of the most infamous "amusement houses. All Swearengen lured women from the East coast with the promise of a career on the stage, but forced them into prostitution after they arrived. Swearengen had a reputation for having a nasty temper and abusing his wife in addition to his employees. An old hand bill advertisement from the Gem included many comics, Vaudeville acts, singers, dancers, and names of women. It is believed that the "theatre" brought in at least $10,000 a night and sometimes ten times that amount.

As we walked towards the door of the Gem, I stopped and could not go in. There was a heavy, dark presence inside and I was not in the mood to deal with it. I believe that some of the negative energies still haunt the site even though the current owners have obviously made an effort to revitalize it.

The **Adams House Museum at 22 Van Buren Street** was once Harris and Anna Franklin's beautiful Queen Anne Victorian style home. The Franklins sold the property to their son Nathan for $1 in 1905, and he later sold it to W.E. and Alice Adams in 1920. W.E.'s daughter died in 1912 from Typhoid Fever, and cancer claimed his wife in 1925 while she was at her daughter's home in California. Her pregnant daughter went into premature labor and died the next day. Adams then married Mary Mastrovich Vicich, age 29, when he was 73 years old, a deed that caused quite a scandal in Deadwood society.

After her husband's death, Mary Adams closed up the home, with all furnishings intact. Today the home has been fully restored with grand money from the City of Deadwood and is a popular tourist attraction. However, visitors may get more than they bargained for while visiting.

During our tour of the home we entered a bedroom in the upper floor. I immediately felt the presence of a male spirit, first at the bed to my left, then I saw him sitting in a rocking chair by the window. The chair moved forward and back on its own accord very slightly. After talking about the room, the tour guide said to catch her after the tour to talk. Apparently she noticed that I saw something in the room.

I approached the guide after the tour was over and explained what I saw. She said that was Mr. Adam's room and that he died in it. She also said that they often see the rocking chair moving and that other psychics have seen him in that room.

One day, she had some friends over for tea in the back yard while the museum was closed. One of the guests saw a man looking out one of the second floor windows, so the guide, along with her friends, went inside the house to investigate. They found nothing. Later, while on a tour of the Adams Museum in town, the guest saw a picture of W.E. Adams and said that was the man she saw in the window. Apparently, other people have seen Adams peering out the same window on other occasions. The guide will probably not mention anything about ghosts unless you bring it up—she is waiting to see what the guests come up with on their own.

Some of the ghosts at the Adams House may not be former residents, however, ghostly activity on the grounds could be from former Ingleside cemetery which used to be nearby.

The **Adams Museum** at 54 Sherman Street was built in 1930 by

William Emery Adams in memory to his first wife and two daughters. The museum has three levels, and has fascinating artifacts and exhibits dedicated to the history of Deadwood. The collection includes the remains of a rare plesiosaur fossil with characteristics of both older and later species.

Once again, I sensed the presence of ghosts on the premises, so asked one of the clerks if they ever experienced ghostly activity there. The clerk told me that whenever W.E. Adam's portrait is removed from its place over the first floor fireplace, lights go on and off and the alarm system acts up. The curator has experienced hearing footsteps in the building when no one is around, and other unexplained noises have occurred there. Apparently W.E. is watching over his creation and doesn't want anything changed.

Wild Bill's Saloon has a ghost that plays the pinball machine in the arcade on the lower level, sometimes for hours on end. Other machines turn off and on, and sometimes light flicker off and on.
Original Site of Saloon No. 10,

Green Door Brothel/Lucky Nugget Gambling Hall is reportedly haunted by a number of uneasy spirits. This is the original location of one of the brothels in Deadwood, so no doubt has some lingering energies. Visitors have seen shadow people, felt unseen people brush against their hair, and have smelled perfume from an unknown source. I didn't stay long, but sensed someone watching me while there.

I was unable to explore the reportedly haunted **Miss Kitty's**, the **Franklin Hotel**, and **Wild West Winner's Casino** in Deadwood, or the **Homestake Visitor Center** and **Black Hills mining Museum,** both in the nearby town of Lead, but plan to on a future visit.

Whether you are interested in ghost hunting or just a great historical place to visit, Deadwood is the perfect place.

For more information about Deadwood, visit the town's official site, www.deadwood.com.

Wild Bill Hickok's final resting place
Photo by Gene P.

CHAPTER 12

76 Famous Haunted Sites to Visit

All of the sites listed in this section are open to the public. Some have tours, others can be reserved for a night's stay, and some are open daily. I have visited most of these sites myself or they have been recommended by other paranormal investigators. Whether you go during the day or night, take your camera with you and take lots of photos!

Houses

The Truman Home, Independence, Missouri
223 N. Main Street, Independence, Missouri

The Truman Home in Independence

Finished in 1886 by Bess Wallace Truman's maternal grandfather George Porterfield. Called "The Summer White House" and where Truman lived after his marriage to Bess. This is where Harry died in 1972. The home is open to the public daily Watch out for Harry himself, who often appears sitting at his desk in the living room or walking outside the home and even around old downtown Independence.

Harry and Bess on their wedding day

Winchester Mystery House- California

525 S Winchester Blvd
San Jose, CA 95128
408-247-2101
www.winchestermysteryhouse.com

Sarah Winchester built what is considered to be the world's oddest mansion because her dead husband told her she and all their descendants were cursed because of the rifle he invented. She was told to build and never stop building. By her death she had 160 rooms in her mansion. Sarah lived alone with her servants, carpenters and the ghosts of all who had died by the Winchester rifle. There have been multiple experiences here by visitors. Open year-round.

Ax Murder House- Villisca Iowa
www.villiscaiowa.com

June 10, 1912 the entire J. B. Moore family were killed by an axe murderer in this house. Visitors have reported hearing sounds of children laughing, and of apparitions caught on film, falling lamps, and objects moving on their own. Listed on the National Registry of Historic Places. Open for daytime tours and overnight stays.

The Whaley House

San Diego, California

www.whaleyhouse.org

619-297-7511

Whaley house admissions are sold at the museum at 2476 San Diego Avenue on Old Town San Diego. According to the Travel Channel's *America's Most Haunted,* the house is the number one most haunted house in the United States. With its history of the suicide of Violet Whaley in 1885 and the hanging of Yankee Jim James Robinson in 1852 on the spot where the house would be built later, it is no wonder it is haunted. I experienced the ghost of a young girl in the back garden while visiting this site in 2004, the apparition of a man in the front hallway, ghosts of children in the upper level of the home, and an angry male spirit near the stairway to the second floor.

Cemeteries

Bachelors Grove Cemetery- Midlothian, Illinois

www.bachelorsgrove.com

Located on the southwest side of Chicago. Over the years this place has been cursed with more than 100 documented reports of paranormal phenomena, from actual apparitions to glowing balls of light.

Hill Park– Independence, Missouri

2099 S Hardy Ave

Independence, MO

The burial site of Frank James and his wife and at least two confederate soldiers. A misty figure is often seen crossing over the hill at sunset. The small cemetery is located at the very back of the park at the top of the hill.

Mound Grove Cemetery– Independence, Missouri
1818 N River Blvd.
Independence, MO
A full-body apparition of a young woman in white floats along the main road inside the cemetery, and a dark figure of a man appears in a dip on the same road. Closes at sunset so don't go after dark.

Woodlawn Cemetery– Independence, Missouri
701 N Noland Rd.
Independence, MO
A very large cemetery where voices and whispering can sometimes be heard. Also thought to be the home of the "Noland Road Lady in Grey," an apparition that walks on Noland Road near the cemetery day or night.

Marie Laveau's Grave– New Orleans, Louisiana
Home of the most famous ghost of Voodoo Queen Marie Laveau, where she can be seen walking in St. Louis Cemetery No.1 even today. I've visited several of the cemeteries in New Orleans and they are ALL haunted!

Hospitals

Glore Psychiatric Museum
3406 Frederick Avenue
St. Joseph, Missouri 64508
www.stjosephmuseum.org/glore.htm
800-530-8866
Chronicles the 130-year history of the "State lunatic Asylum No.2"

which is haunted by several restless spirits. Tours available.

Waverly Hills Sanatorium– Louisville, Kentucky
502-933-2142
www.therealywaverlyhills.com
A TB sanatorium opened in 1910. There have been many sightings of ghosts including a small girl running, and a boy with a leather ball Also smells of baking waft thru the air. On the fifth floor disembodied voices demand visitors to "get out". Open for tours and investigators.

Bed and Breakfast/Inns

Myrtles Plantation– Louisiana
7747 U S Hwy 61
St. Francisville, LA 70775
800-809-0565
www.themyrtlesplantation.com
Restaurant and tours. As you visit this 1776 plantation built by General
David Bradford don't be surprised if you see full-body apparitions or handprints in the mirrors, hear footsteps on the stairs, and more. Reported to be one of the most haunted houses in the United States.

Lemp Mansion Restaurant and Inn—St. Louis, Missouri
3322 DeMerit Place
St. Louis, Missouri 63118
314-664-8024
www.lempmansion.com
Considered one of the ten most haunted places in America, this

1868 mansion built by Jacob Feickert, and purchased by William Lemp in 1876. Several deaths occurred in the house due to natural causes and suicides and many ghost stories abound about this place. There are six ghosts here. Open to the public as a bed and breakfast, restaurant, and dinner theatre. Paranormal tours are available.

Lizzie Bordon Bed and Breakfast Museum– Fall River, Mass.
92 Second Street
Fall River, Massachusetts 02721
508-605-6333
www.lizzie-bordon.com
A beautiful fully restored Victorian home and site of the gruesome axe murders of Andrew Bordon in the sitting room and Abby Bordon in her bedroom on August 4, 1892. Lizzie Bordon, daughter of Andrew, was the prime suspect but was found not guilty at her trial. Several paranormal investigators have captured ghosts on film and EVPs on recorders. Sleep over night here or take one of the daily tours.

Hotels and Restaurants

The Stanley Hotel– Colorado
333 E Wonder View Ave
Estes Park, CO 80517-9665
970-586-3371
www.stanleyhotel.com
This very haunted hotel, which opened in 1909 inspired the Stephen King novel "The Shining." Book room 217, which is where King stayed or any where on floor 4, which was the servant's quarters. A servant was seriously injured in that room in a fire and later died on the property. Flora Stanley, the wife of the hotel owner is

among the many ghosts that haunt the place. During my visit in 2011 a ghost pushed me in the back twice. I sensed three active spirits on the property, and one very dark energy on the fourth floor. Open year-round.

The Bullock Hotel

633 Main Street
Deadwood, SD

The Bullock is a massive stone structure was built by entrepreneurs Seth Bullock and Sol Star in 1894-96. Bullock had been sheriff in Lewis and Clark County, Montana before his arrival in Deadwood. Bullock's grandson described him as "Tall, with steely gray eyes and an imposing appearance that commanded respect. It was said that he could outstare a mad cobra or a rogue elephant."

The hotel has been restored to its Italianate Victorian style, and is worth visiting even if you don't care to see a ghost, which you likely will. Seth Bullock's spirit is very active in the hotel. Take along a night vision camera and you won't be disappointed. Make reservations at www.historicbullock.com

The Hotel Savoy- Kansas City, Missouri

219 W 9th Street
Kansas City, MO
www.hotelsavoy.net
816-842-3575

1888 brick building haunted by several ghosts who were upset by renovations in the 1980s. Watch out for Betsy Ward, who died in a bathtub in the 1880s and Fred Lightner haunting his former apartment. Open to the public.

The Hyatt– Kansas City, Missouri

2345 McGee Street
Kansas City, Missouri
816-421-1234
www.crowncenter.hyatt.com

Site of the terrible Hyatt Regency walkway collapse in 1981 which killed 114 people during a tea dance. One of the floors is closed due to multiple sightings of ghosts there, however ghosts have been spotted in the ballroom, elevator, lobby, and on several floors. The staff does not talk about it, so just keep your eye out if you spend the night there.

The 1886 Crescent Hotel and Spa– Eureka Springs, Arkansas

75 Prospect Avenue
Eureka Springs, AR 72632
877-342-9766
www.crescent-hotel.com

Room 218 is the most active spot for paranormal activity, likely because one of the Irish stone masons working on the structure in the 1880s fell to his death here. However, I saw a ghost cat in the lobby who walked through the glass doors, and other people have reported sightings, loud noises, and poltergeist activity throughout the hotel. Two friends of mine even had UFO sightings from their balconies, and another saw a apparition at the end of the hallway. Definitely worth a visit.

The Sagamore– Bolton Landing, New York

110 Sagamore Road
Bolton Landing, NY 12814
833-385-6221
www.thesagamore.com

Located on a private island on Lake George. While dining in the Trillium you may be visited by a couple who descend from the second floor and take a seat in the restaurant's reception room. Or visit the hotel's second restaurant, Mr. Brown's, where you may see an apparition of a tall woman dressed in white evening attire.

Jekyll Island Club Hotel– Jekyll Island, Georgia

371 Riverview Drive

Jekyll Island, GA 61527

www.jekyllclub.com

Samuel Spencer still haunts his room at the hotel. Spencer was president of the Southern Railroad Company and had a morning routine of reading the Wall Street Journal while drinking coffee. He died in 1906 in a railroad accident, but still drinks his morning coffee in his room today.

The Myrtles Plantation

Louisiana

Stay the night and experience the presence of the dead as they walk around the Myrtles. Saint Francisville is located in West Feliciana Parish Louisiana, which is a small town on the Mississippi River. John James Audubon (Birds of America Collection) created over 80 of his beautiful watercolors at this site. There are seven Magnificent Plantation homes open for public tours and a restaurant on site, but The Myrtles Plantation is the one not to miss. You may see the ghost of Chloe hanging around, among others. Open year-round. Visit Myrtlesplantation.com for more information.

Hawthorne Hotel

Salem, Mass

Built in 1925 four tourists, the Hawthorne hotel is named after

Salem's most famous resident Nathaniel Hawthorne, who grew up there as a child. People often smell apples on the site, even though the orchard owned by Bridget Bishop is long gone.

The hotel is reportedly haunted by long gong ship captains who participated in the meetings of the Salem Marine Society, which operated at this site in the early 1900s. The building was torn down to allow for construction of the hotel.

The restaurant in the hotel has a large ship's wheel as part of its nautical theme. Many people have reported seeing the wheel turn on its own with no explanation.

An employee reports that in a room called the "Lower Deck," furniture will be rearranged shortly after he left and returned shortly after. The employee left the hotel and refused to return.

Rooms reported to be haunted are 612 and 325, where unexplained events occur. Guests report being touched in the middle of the night, presences felt at the end of their beds, and objects missing or moved.

Theatres

The Music Hall- Kansas City, Missouri

301 W 13th Street

Kansas City, Missouri

If you attend a concert there, watch out for several ghosts who haunt, especially inside the theatre where they sit in chairs. Most witnesses think they are looking at a real person until the apparition disappears. No tours are available.

Landers Theater– Springfield, Missouri

311 E Walnut

Springfield, Missouri 65806

www.springfieldlittetheatre.org
417-869-3869 (office)
Built in 1909 and still used as a civic theatre today, the theater has a history of tragic deaths and ghosts that haunt. The beautiful theatre is on the National Register of Historic Places.

Lincoln Theater- Decatur, Illinois

Listen as you enter the theater and you may hear ghostly footsteps, inexplicable sounds, and even feel icy cold chills that appear and disappear without explanation. Lincoln Theater is a glorious place—come meet restless phantoms of those whose lives ended on this spot, some before the theater existed.

Bobby Mackey's Music World-Wilder, Kentucky

Occult rituals, trials, strange visits to women five months pregnant and many other delights visit you in this strange house with just ads strange a history.

Coleman Theatre– Miami, Oklahoma

On Historic Route 66 in northeastern Oklahoma. A beautiful restored theatre, the Coleman is famous for its ghostly residents. The theatre is haunted by a little boy named Stuart, who likes to hold on to lady's legs, making them cold. You can also smell men's cologne and pipes at times, and walk into cold spots.

Syracuse Landmark Theater-Syracuse, New York

362 S Salina St, Syracuse, NY
315-475-7980
www.landmarktheatre.org
This 1928 theatre was renovated in 1978 and shortly after the apparition of a pale lady, and an electrician named Oscar Rau started

haunting it. The theater is on the National Register of Historic Places.

King Opera House

427 Main Street, Van Buren, AR

Built in the late 19th century and part of an Historic District, this Victorian era structure is still in use today. It is said that a young actor planned to run away with the daughter of a local doctor, but before they could leave the train station someone saw them and informed the girls father, who was the local Doctor. The Doctor whipped the man to death and the daughter ran off, never to be seen again. The actor's ghost was first seen by a set designer during the first production of a play at the newly reopened theatre in 1979. The ghost materializes dressed in a top had and Victorian style coat and cape.

Battlefields/Forts

Gettysburg Battlefield– Southern Pennsylvania

Gettysburg National Military Park

97 Taneytown Rd.

Gettysburg, PA 17325

717-334-1124

www.nps.gov/gett

The bloodiest battle of the Civil War was fought here July 1 –3, 1863. Over 51,000 soldiers were killed, wounded, or captured on this spot. The battle spilled over in to the town, where ghostly apparitions of men, women, and children have been sighted. The battlefield is one of the most haunted sites in America. Don't be surprised if you see actors in uniform only to find out that they can walk through walls and trees.

Antietam Battlefield, Maryland
5831 Dunker Church Road
Sharpsburg, MD 21782
www.nps.gov/anti
The second bloodiest battle of the Civil War was fought here on September 17, 1832. 23,000 soldiers died on that day, which lead to President Lincoln's issuance of the Emancipation Proclamation. Visitors report seeing orbs and apparitions, hearing gunfire and cannon, and seeing strange blue lights in the battlefield, nearby houses and the cemetery.

Chickamauga, and Chattanooga National Military Park– Eastern Tennessee and northern Georgia.
423-821-7786
www.nps.gov/chch
Chickamauga Battlefield is located near Fort Oglethorpe. Lookout Mountain Battlefield is located at the end of East Brow Road near Point Park. Said to be very haunted by visitors ever since the Civil war battle in September of 1863. Visitors have taken photographs of ghost horses and men, and have seen apparitions of tall, dark entities.

The Alamo– San Antonio, Texas
300 Alamo Plaza
San Antonio, Texas 78299
www.thealamo.org
Since March 6, 1836 the ghosts of Jim Bowie and Davy Crockett along with many others have purportedly haunted this site.

Little Bighorn– Montana
Little Bighorn National Monument

Exit 510 of I-90 Hwy 212
Crow Agency, MT 59022
406-638-3217 www.nps.gov.libi

The site of Custer's Last Stand in June 1876, and where reports of shadows, mists, fog, apparitions, and Indian chanting and war cries can be seen and heard here. I experienced the presence of hundreds of spirits at this location.

Valley Forge– Pennsylvania
Valley Forge Convention and Visitors Bureau
600 W Germantown Pike, Suite 130
Plymouth Meeting, PA 19462
800-441-3549
www.valleyforge.org
The site where General Washington's Continental Army camped for six months from December 1777 to June 1778 during severe conditions and bitter, long winter, and where may ghosts have been seen and heard.

Fort Osage-Missouri
107 Osage Street
Sibley, MO 64088
816-650-3278
www.fortosagehs.com
The second U.S. outpost built following the Louisiana Purchase, a site chosen by William Clark in 1808. The Fort housed soldiers guarding the new territory and acted as a stop for settlers heading West. The current fort is an exact duplicate of the original. Current workers and visitors report sightings and interaction with soldiers and Indians.

Cold Harbor Battlefield- Richmond, Virginia
Five miles southeast of Mechanicsville on route 156
804-226-1981 www.nps.gov/rich

Ulysses S Grant was in command at this battle that was fought between May 31 and June 12, 1864. 16,000 men died or were wounded. Visitors report encounters with apparitions of solders, strange lights, the sounds of horses and cannon, and orbs and mist captured on film.

When going to a battlefield, check ahead for opening hours and directions. Don't depend on GPS– sometimes it is not correct.

Schools

Note: get permission before going into closed or non-public buildings.

Central Missouri State University– Warrensburg, Missouri
Ghosts have been reported in Deimer Hall, Hawkins Hall, Houts/Hosey Hall, north Ellis, and Yeater Hall. Yeater is the most famous for apparitions—I know first hand since I lived in that hall. Besides things happening inside, you may also get a glimpse of a female ghost in a third-floor window. Get permission before you go inside since these are dormitories.

Kansas State University– Manhattan, Kansas
Pi Kappa Phi fraternity and Gamma Phi Beta sorority houses are reportedly haunted by ghosts.

Stephens College-Columbia, Missouri
Senior Hall, where the ghost of Sarah June Wheeler searches for the ghost of Confederate Soldier Isaac Johnson. They both perished on the site or nearby.

St. Joseph's college– Emmitsburg, Maryland

A former women's college that was used a hospital during the Civil War. The apparition of Saint Mother Seton is often seen in the corridors accompanied by the ghost of a doctor.

Lourdes High School– Chicago, Illinois

4034 West 57th Street, Chicago, Illinois

Students, teachers and visitors report hearing music, talking, and ghostly footsteps when the halls are quiet.

Decatur High School– Decatur, Alabama

Apparitions floating down the hall and footsteps in silent corridors have been reported by students and teachers here.

The Music Academy– Independence, Missouri

Look up at the third floor windows from the street where you might catch a glimpse of a young girl ghost. She has been reported by multiple witnesses.

Henderson State University– Arkadelphia, Arkansas

Home of "The Black Lady," a ghost of a woman who returns during dances at the school and may be the ghost of a young woman who committed suicide there.

Reynolds College– Denver, Colorado

The ghost of Madge Reynolds has been seen in her bedroom in this historic house, where she died after returning from a horseback ride with her lover Fred Bonfils.

Eastern Illinois University– Charleston, Illinois

The ghost of Mary, a counselor who was killed by a custodian on the 3rd floor of Pemberton Hall in the 1920s, often drifts from room to room checking on the girls there.

Gorman School– Lebec, California

The school was built on the site of a farm where a 12-year-old girl was killed by her father's tractor. Her body was laid to rest under the state in the school auditorium and often appears to people and sometimes speaks to them.

Prisons and Jails

Alcatraz-San Francisco California
www.nps.gov/alcatraz

First a fortress (1850-1934), then a prison (1934-63), and the American Indian occupation (1964–71). From its naming in 1775 Alcatraz has been host to prisoners- Confederate soldiers to our countries most hardened criminals like Al Capone and Robert Stroud. Tours available to the public. Only accessible by ferry.

1859 Jackson County Jail– Independence, Missouri

Includes the Marshal's House, which is also haunted. Former housing to thousands of men, women, and child prisoners during the Civil War and after, including Frank James and William Clark Quantrill until it closed in 1933. Much ghostly activity has been reported here and we experienced this during our own visit. Apparitions appear, ghosts fight with each other, cold spots abound, and visitors report invisible hands touching their shoulders. Open to the public year round. I don't recommend this for children due to the high likelihood of a paranormal encounter.

Eastern State Penitentiary– Pennsylvania

2124 Fairmount Ave.

Philadelphia, PA 19130
215-236-5111
www.easternstate.org
A massive 1829 gothic structure in Philadelphia's Fairmount neighborhood and former home to Al Capone, Slick Willie Sutton, and thousands of other prisoners who lived and died there. U.S. National Register of Historic Places. Open to the public for tours year -round.

The Tower of London
0870 756 6060
www.hrp.org.uk
This 1,000 year old structure is home to the ghosts of Henry VI, Thomas a Becket, Sir Walter Raleigh and Anne Boleyn, who all died there. Public executions were held on Tower Green, including two of Henry VIII's wives, Anne Boleyn and Catherine Howard. The White Tower built by William the Conqueror around 1100 now houses a display of armory. I encountered multiple spirits in the tower while visiting it in 2005. Open year-round to the public.

Other Famous Haunted Places

(Not in Alphabetical Order)

Bell Witch Cave- Adams, Tennessee
The Bell Witch Cave & Canoe Rental
430 Keysburg Road, Adams, TN 37010
615-696-3055
www.bellwitchcave.com
The story starts in 1817 with the family of a local farmer named John Bell. John Bell was plagued for by a mysterious and violent spirit for nearly four years. The haunting included spectral crea-

tures, disembodied voices, unbelievable violence and even resulted in the death of John Bell, all at the hands of the infamous Bell Witch, many of whom believe moved to this cave after leaving the Bell residence.

Dracula's Castle or Castle Bran- Wallachia, Transylvania
Situated in the remote Carpathian mountains in Romania, Bran Castle was home to Vlad the Impaler, who impaled thousands of victims at a time during his reign of terror. Very difficult to access, so only the very adventurous should plan to visit.

The Catacombs– Paris, France
The home to thousands of the dead since the late 1800s and the site of many ghostly experiences. Do not go without a guide or you risk getting lost forever in the maze of catacombs under the city. Check with local tour operators for information. The entrance to the Paris Catacombs is located across the street from the Denfert- Rochereau Metro station.

Lalaurie House– New Orleans, Louisiana
1140 Royal Street
New Orleans, Louisiana
Visitors report seeing and hearing the long-dead slaves and original owners of this home as they frantically try to put out the fire that killed them long ago. Open to the public.

Underground Vaults- Edinburgh, Scotland
Under the streets of the city lie vaults that were used 200 years ago by businesses, residences, and workshops. Later, the homeless used the vaults and it is suspected that the famous Burke and Hare killed homeless and sold the bodies to the teaching hospitals. The ghosts

here are very aggressive and have actually caused physical harm to people. Not for children.

The Coliseum– Rome, Italy

This 2000-year-old structure was home to Gladiator battles to the death, and religious persecution where thousands lost their lives when attacked by lions and tigers. Visitors have reported cold spots, being touched or pushed, hearing talking, and crying along with animal noises.

The New Castle (Black Gate and Keep)- England

Newcastle-upon-Tyne
0191 231 2700
www.newcaslte-antiquaries.org.
Castle built by Henry 11 in 1168– 78
Hundreds of dead were moved from a graveyard in 1172 in order to allow for the new castle to be built. Many paranormal investigators have reported seeing spirits here. Open for tours.

Edinburgh Castle– Scotland

www.edinburghcastle.gov.uk
A fortress built in the 12th century, home of dungeons used for torture and imprisonment over the centuries and home to spirits now. The vaults used to quarantine victims of the plague are reportedly haunted, and visitors often hear the screams of spirits. Open to the public.

Chillingham Castle– England

2 Market Street
Alnwick, Northumberland NE66 65N
01668 215 359

www.chillingham-catle.com
Visit this 13th century castle and you may see the "blue boy" who haunts the Pink Room where is body was found bricked up in a 10-foot thick wall, Lady Mary, or hear the cries of the tortured souls in the dungeons or of the eight executions of famous people who were hung, drawn and quartered. Open to the public May—October.

Union Station- Kansas City, Missouri
30 West Pershing, Rd.
Kansas City, MO 64105
816-221-5111
Site of the Kansas City Massacre. Built in 1914, Union Station was once a thriving railway station for passengers and freight. Now fully restored and open to the public. Ghosts carrying bags have been reported in the old lobby, on the railroad tracks, in Pierpont's restaurant and in the Historical Room above Pierpont's. I heard a ghost in the ladies room, and saw an apparition in the main lobby while visiting in 2009. This was the site of the 1933 Massacre of federal agents by Pretty Boy Floyd, Vernon Miller, and Adam Richetti during a failed attempt to free prisoner Frank Nash. Open year-round.

The Queen Mary– Long Beach, California
1126 Queen's Highway
Long Beach, CA 90802
877-342-0742
This 1936 ship has been turned into a hotel for guests to the Long Beach area. The ship made over 1,000 Atlantic crossings and it is estimated that almost 50 people lost their lives on the vessel. During WWII the ocean liner collided with the Curacao from Britain, which was split in two. Because of strict orders the Queen Mary could not stop to rescue the 338 men who perished as a result of the accident.

Open to the public for tours and overnight stays in the hotel.

The White House– Washington, DC
It is rumored that at least 20 ghost haunt the White House, with Abe Lincoln's bedroom being the most haunted. Even Queen Elizabeth **saw** the ghost of Lincoln during a visit there. Ghosts have been reported in all rooms and on the lawn, but the most haunted rooms are not open to the public. To get tickets, contact your member of Congress and request tickets to tour the White House several months in advance of your visit. Tours are self-guided and begin at 7:30 a.m. and run until 11:30 a.m. Tuesday through Saturday. Call 202-456-7041.

The Capital Building—Washington, DC
Constitution Avenue.
www.visitthecapital.gov
Open from 8:30 a.m. to 4:30 p.m. Monday—Saturday except for holidays. Reservations must be made in advance through your representative or senator, or book online at the capital website (above). Visit the Capital Building while in DC and you may see the ghost of John Adams walking around along with Vice-President Henry Wilson, President James Garfield, General Jon Alexander, a custodian, and others. A black cat (called the Demon Cat) is sometimes sighted before a tragedy or administration changes.

Old Salem
Salem, Massachusetts
Site of the Salem witch trials in 1692 where the court hung 20 women and crushed one man to death with stones. Reported haunted sites are the Ward House which is haunted by the ghosts of Sheriff Corwin and Giles Corey. Corwin is buried in the cellar. The YMCA

pool is haunted by a swimmer who died there. The Hawthorne Hotel elevator and sixth floor are haunted by murdered ghosts, and Gallows Hill is reported to be haunted by the "witches" who died there. The House of the Seven Gables is also haunted. During a visit by the QUEST team we encountered full apparitions in windows of buildings, and at the old jail. During a walk through the town graveyard a ghost yanked my purse off of me so hard that it broke the leather strap in half.

Plymouth, Massachusetts

Reported to be haunted at Clapp Park, Cordage Park, the Spooner House Museum, and the State Forest. While driving the streets in Plymouth, sometimes spelled Plymouth, I felt many spirits in the town. No wonder, this is one of the oldest settlements in the U.S. The Spooner House Museum is worth visiting, haunted or not.

Tombstone, Arizona

Reported to be one of the most haunted towns in the world. Tombstone was a boomtown from 1877 1889 when silver was discovered and the site of many bloody shootouts, including the famous O.K. Corral incident. The ghost of Marshal Fred White has been seen. White was the first marshal of Tombstone. A man in a long black frock coat has been seen near the site where Virgil Earp was ambushed and shot in the arm. Also spied on the streets is a woman in a long white dress. More than 40 men died in fires in 1881 and 1882 and some have been seen walking the streets while the unexplained smell of smoke is noted. Visitors also report getting ghosts on camera.

Clark Street– Chicago, Illinois

Site of the famous Saint Valentine's Day Massacre in 1929 and the site where 812 people died under the Clark Street bridge when the

Eastland boat capsized in 1915. Cries can still be heard under the bridge.

Mammoth Cave National Park– Kentucky

The largest natural cave in the world. Over 150 reports of ghostly activity since the cave's discovery in 1978 and very active today. At least five spirits haunt the site.

San Antonio, Texas

Another very haunted site, San Antonio is one of the oldest cities in the U.S. and has a long, rich history. The Alamo, the Railroad tracks, the Sheraton Gunter Hotel, and Menger Hotel are reported to be haunted. After the battle of the Alamo, Mexican troops saw full apparitions and heard them yelling for the men to leave. Moaning sounds and shadows still appear at this site. Just south of San Antonio near the San Juan Mission is the site of the most famous ghost legend in Texas. Ten children were killed when a train hit a school bus in the 1930s or 1940s, and since then ghost children push cars uphill at this intersection. Supposedly, if you stop your car right over the railroad tracks and shift into neutral, the car will be pushed out of the way uphill by the ghosts of the children. A friend of mine visited the spot, sprinkled baby powder on the car and stopped her car on the tracks. Within a couple of minutes the car started moving, while it was off and in park, across the tracks. A child dressed in a pinafore dress appeared in the rear-view mirror. My friend got out of the car and found hand prints of children on the back.

The Real 'Blair Witch' Ghosts, Burkittsville, Maryland

The movie was fiction, but the site is not.

Since 1735, people have been talking about the strange goings on around Burkittsville . According to some the community has been terrorized by the "Schnellgeister," the German word for "fast sprit." Described as half-reptile with octopus limbs and half bird with a metallic beak and sharp teeth, the "Snallygaster" can fly, capture people, and suck their blood. Other animal spirits and ghosts haunt the town, which housed 17 Civil War hospitals. The hospitals were homes and the old tannery used for the purpose. Stories of Civil War ghosts abound. The tannery site is haunted today. If you park your car there overnight you may find footprints from soldier's boots on it in the morning.

Courthouse Exchange Restaurant– Independence, Missouri
113 W Lexington
Independence, Missouri
Haunted by prankster ghost children in the bar and restaurant who are very active. The manager told me the ghosts play a "dime game" and leave several dimes, always face-up, on tables and the bar every morning and often leave the TV turned to the cartoon channel, which is normally on news stations on in the morning. A ghost girl and boy have been spotted by patrons on a number of occasions. (see my book Haunted Independence for more information)

The Catacombs
Kansas City, MO
816-474-3845
A haunted attraction in the West bottoms of Kansas City, Missouri, this site is haunted by a previous owner who tragically died in a horrible accident at the site, and likely other spirits. A worker at the site witnessed the death of the owner, but was saved by an unseen force that pushed him out of the way of the deadly cable that killed the owner only a couple of seconds earlier. Paranormal groups have

investigated this site and have obtained EVPs and heard unexplained noises. Witnesses report seeing foggy apparitions and dark shadow people who disappear. Open to the public during the fall season as a haunted attraction, but don't be surprised if you see a real ghost.

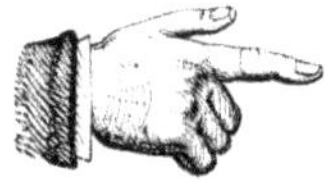

TIP:

Check on eBay (ebay.com) and Craig's List (www.craigslist.com) for great deals on cameras and other equipment. Be sure to get a warranty.

CHAPTER 13

Paranormal Radio and TV Shows

The following are current radio and television shows that often cover ghosts and the paranormal.

Paranormal Radio

KGRA—Digital Broadcasting radio network has numerous shows with hosts including Richard Dolan, Mack Maloney, Lorin Cutts, Race Hobbs, Royce Fitzgerald, Chase Kloetske, Margie Kay. Steve Hudgeons, and others covering UFO and Paranormal topics. KGRA is the official MUFON network. Listen live at www.kgraradio.com. There is a live chat room available as well.

Un-X News Radio with Margie Kay. Margie interviews world experts on Paranormal and UFO topics weekly. Visit www.unxnews.com for more information.

The Richard Dolan Show Saturdays 8—11 pm EST. Richard is among the world's leading UFO researchers. www.kgraradio.com

Eye Witness Radio with Race and Royce, interviewing top U.F.O. researchers Thursdays 7—9 pm Eastern on kgraradio.com

Project White Paper with Chase Klotezke. Paranormal researchers and authors. Thursdays 9 pm EST www.chasekloetzke.com or kgraradio.com

Coast to Coast AM with hosts George Noory, Ian Punnett and Art Bell. Currently the most popular talk show on the paranormal. The website iswww.coasttocoastam.com. Live streaming audio (and video) available. Also on XM radio.

MUFON Radio and Texas UFO Radio with Steve Hudgeons. kgraradio.com

Nightwatch with host Todd Sheets, is the home of the Nightwatchers paranormal investigative group.
www.nightwatchradio.com. Live streaming audio, and through affiliates.

Nightsearch is MUFON Tennessee state director Eddie Middleton's popular paranormal show in the South. The website is www.nightsearch.net. The call-in line is 901-365-1430.

Darkness Radio with David Schrader. www.ktlkfm.com or www.darkessradio.com

Sightings with Jeff Rense is one of the most popular and long-running paranormal radio shows. Real audio and archives are at www.sightings.com.

Paranormal Awareness radio show with author Dr. Hans Holzer. www.paranormalawarenessradioshow.net.

Anomaly Radio with multiple hosts and various topics. www.anomalyradio.com

PsiTalk: Internet web station hosting Dreamland, Ghostly Talk, Jerry pippin, Strange Days, A.P.S.R. talk show, Coast to Coast, and more. www.psitalk.com

Alabama ParaSpiritual Research Radio with Dr .Jimmy Lowery and Heather Lowery. www.apsrradio.

Paranormal Alaska Radio with Neelie and Tony of IOPIA.

www.blocktalkradio.com/alaskaparanormal

Crossroads Paranormal Radio with hosts Kris and Sheila. www.insightbb.com/~crossroadsparanormal/cpr.htm

Tuesday After Twilight international paranormal talk radio. www.tuesdayaftertwilight.com

Ghostly Talk on Sunday nights with Doug "Skizz" and Scott L. . www.ghostlytalk.com

Planet Paranormal talk radio with multiple hosts and programs. www.planetparanormal.com

White Noise Radio paranormal talk radio from the UK. www.whitenoiseradio.webs.com

The Unexplained World talk radio show with Ed and Annette. Www.theunexplainedworld.com.

The Paracast talk radio with Gene Steinberg and Greg Bishop. www.theparacast.com.

Paranormal TV Shows

Ghost Hunters TV Show with Jason and Grant and the Atlantic Paranormal Society (TAPS) team. On the SyFy channel. www.syfy.com/gh

Ghost Adventures TV show with Zac Bagans, Nick Groff, and Aaron Goodwin investigate while being locked up at the location overnight. On the Travel Channel. www.travelchannel.com/TV_Shows/Ghost_Adventures.

Paranormal State TV show with Ryan Buell and the Paranormal Research Society. Airs on A&E. www.aetv.com/paranormal-state

Ghost Lab TV show with Brad and Barry Klinge and Everyday

Paranormal. Airs on the Discovery channel. www.disc.discovery.com/tv/ghost-lab/ghost-lab.html
Ghost Hunters International TV show is a spin-off of Ghost Hunters. On the SyFy channel.
Most Haunted TV show on the Travel Channel with Yvette Fielding and a team of investigators. www.livingtv.co.uk/shows/most-haunted-the-live-series.

Paranormal Cops TV reality show with real-life Chicago police officers by day who work as paranormal investigators at night. www.aetv.com/paranormal-cops/index.jsp

Paranormal TV from The Unexplained World. Live broadcasts

Resources

Public libraries are a wealth of information for research. If you need to check the history of a site, check your library for newspaper articles and books on the history of the area.

Old newspaper archives can be found at Newspaperarchive.com for a fee, or visit Google News Archives at news.google.com/archivesearch, and XooxieAnswers.com for free archive searches.

For family information and photos visit Ancestry.com, Genealogy.com, and cyndislist.com for information on local families.

For Civil War Records, visit www.nors.us/civilrecords and for Revolutionary War Records visit www.dar.org.

Visit your local county website for property and land information, vital statistics, criminal, and tax information, which may provide more information about the site you are investigating.

CHAPTER 14

Resources

Meditation CDs:
Rhythmic Medicine (Janalea Hoffman)
www.rhythmicmedicine.com 913-851-5100 or
EOC Institute: www.eocinstitute.org or
Meditation Transformation :www.meditationtransformation.com

Laser Thermometers:
Laser Thermometers: Laserthermometers.net 1-800-334-9291
Professional Equipment:
www.professionalequipment.com 1-800-334-9291

Digital Voice Recorders:
www.recorders.com 1-800-512-251-1302
www.shop.com

Infrared Monoculars and Binoculars:
www.nightvisionbinoculars.com 1-866-310-8398
www.shop.com

Digital still and video cameras:
Sony: www.sonystyle.com 1-877-865-7669
Canon: www.usa.canon.com
Kodak: www.kodak.com

Reviews of Digital Cameras: *Check this out before you buy!*
www.reviews.cnet.com

Hypnosis Certification: And a list of certified hypnotists
www.ozarkmt.com

EMF Detectors:
http://www.trifield.com/EMF_meter.htm
www.ghosthunterstore.com
www.lessemf.com

To increase your psychic abilities, learn to dowse or go on a ghost hunting expedition: Check with QUEST for classes held every fall in Kansas City and for scheduled conference lectures and ghost hunts. E-mail: margiekay06@yahoo.com

Join the Quest Investigation Group chat list at http://tech.groups.yahoo.com/group/questinvestigationgroup Free to join.

Pendulums and dowsing rods:
Witches' Glen: www.witchesglen.com

Wind Meters:
Windtronic: www.windmeter.net
Speed Tech: www.speedtech.com 703-430-8055

EMF Detectors:
http://www.trifield.com/EMF_meter.htm
www.ghosthunterstore.com
www.lessemf.com

Ghost Hunting Software:
www.simplyghost.com

Increase your psychic abilities, learn to dowse or go on a ghost hunting expedition: Check with QUEST for classes held every fall in Kansas City and for her scheduled conference lectures and ghost hunts. Website: www.margiekay.com or e-mail margiekay06@yahoo.com

CHAPTER 15

Glossary of Paranormal Terms

Agent: A person who is the focus of poltergeist activity.

Akashic Record: Mystical knowledge encoded in a non-physical plane. Also described as a library Accessible through astral projection or consciousness projection, some clairvoyants believe that the Akashic Record is held in the rings of Saturn.

Amulet: An object, such as a stone, or necklace thought to have the power to offer protection.

Anomalous: 1: inconsistent with or deviating from what is usual, normal, or expected: irregular, unusual.

Apparition: The full or partial visible manifestation of a spirit, which often appears as translucent or foggy, but may also appear solid.

Asport: A physical object that a spirit teleports to a different location or makes disappear.

Astral Body: The body that a living person uses to travel in during an involuntary "out of body" experience, often while sleeping or in a deep trance or during intentional "astral projection." While in the astral body, the person can feel objects and hear and see very well.

Astral Plane: A higher dimensional plane that the astral body travels in, and may also be where ghosts exist or travel through.

Astral Projection: When a person purposely and intentionally leaves their physical body via the astral body.

Aura: The field of energy, thought to come from the physical and subtle bodies of a living person, animal, or plant. The auras of people are more complex than other living things. Some clairvoyants can see one or more layers of the aura.

Automatic Writing: The ability to channel a spirit or entity by writing messages without conscious control or memory of what is being written by using a pen or pencil, or typing.

Automatism: An unconscious or involuntary muscular movement theoretically caused by spirits.

Autoscopy: The image of one's body looking back at themselves from a position outside the physical body.

Ball Lightning: A rare form of lighting in the shape of a ball, thought to consist of ionized gas or plasma. Ball lightning only lasts a short time.

Banshee: The wailing spirit that appears to be in two places at the same time, and is an omen of death.

Channeling: The method a medium uses to contact and relay information to others, often during a séance session.

Clairaudient: A person who can hear voices of the dead or other sounds, or hear a living person speaking who is not within normal hearing range.

Clairsentient: A psychic who can sense or "feel" the presence of something or someone, or who knows something without seeing or hearing it.

Clairvoyant: A person who can see ghosts, see through walls, see far-away locations or past and future events by using their mind or "third eye".

Cold spot: A specific area that is much colder than the surrounding space. An authentic cold spot cannot be explained by drafts, air ducts, or other natural phenomena.

Collective Apparition: When more than one person sees the same apparition or phenomena, often from different locations.

Crisis Apparition: An apparition that is seen just prior to an event that could cause serious injury or death.

Déjà vu: The impression of having experienced something before, often with complete recollection of what is coming next.

Demon: An evil entity, often associated with demonic possession, who has never incarnated into a human body, and who purportedly works with the devil. It is unusual to encounter a real demon.

Digital Camera: A type of filmless camera used successfully in ghost hunting. It is believed that digital cameras capture more of the light spectrum than is normally seen by the human eye.

Direct Voice Phenomenon or DVP: Voice of a spirit that is audible to all or most people doing an investigation or séance.

Doppelganger: The exact mirror image of a person, which is considered to be very negative. May also be the same person in a different time.

Dowsing: The ancient practice of using a pendulum, L-rods, Y-branches, or similar device in order to access the super-conscious mind and locate minerals, water, lost items, or in this case, ghosts.

Draft: Some investigators have success hearing spirits speak through things that cause draft such as chimneys, vents, or tubes.

Earthbound: A ghost or spirit that was unable to cross over to the other side at the time of death and is stuck on earth.

Ectoplasm: An ethereal substance associated with spirit manifestations.

Electronic Voice Phenomenon: Sounds or voices of a paranormal source, usually obtained on a voice recorder or video tape.

Elementals: Earth spirits, sprites, fairies, elves, gnomes, and other non-human beings that may exist on the earth and are inter-dimensional.

EMF Detector or Magnetometer: A device used to detect electro-magnetic fields.

Entity: A being other than a living human being, often associated with dark energies.

Extra Sensory Perception or ESP: Perception by means other than the five physical senses, otherwise known as the "Sixth Sense," including clairvoyance, clairaudience, and clairsentience.

Exorcism: A ritual used to remove or banish entities thought to possess person or animal, or haunt a location. Often a member of a religious organization will perform the ritual.

Full Apparition: When a spirit manifests as a full or nearly full body, either transparent or solid.

Gauss meter: See EMF

GESP: General Extrasensory Perception. ESP in which it is unclear whether the results are due to telepathy, precognition, clairvoyance, or retrocognition.

Ghost: The apparition or spirit of a deceased person, which may or may not be visible.

Ghost Hunting: A controlled research project in which various methods and equipment are used to investigate reports of ghosts and hauntings.

Haunting: Recurring ghostly phenomena associated with spirits. Hauntings are usually associated with locations rather than persons.

Hellhound or Black Dog: A ghostly dog that appears just before death. Also associated with negative spirit hauntings.

Incubus: A demon in male form who lies upon sleeping women.

Kinetic Energy: Energy needed to force an object at rest into motion. Objects in motion have kinetic energy. (Also see Telekinesis)

Kirlian Photography: a form of photogram made with a high voltage, named after Semyon Kirlian who accidentally discovered that if an object on a photographic plate is connected to a source of high voltage it will show the aura.

Ley Lines: Theoretical lines, possibly related to the magnetic fields of the earth, connecting ancient and modern sites around the world. Alfred Watkins first used the term in the 1920s after noticing that many structures could be connected by straight lines, and that some had relationships to star alignments. Intersections of these lines are said to have spiritual energy and certain structures are often found at these intersections. Some clairvoyants can see the ley lines, and they are often located by dowsing.

Levitation: To lift or raise an object in apparent defiance of gravity.

Matrix: A web-like structure, only visible to psychics, which connects everything in the universe and provides information to those who can tap into it. Not yet fully understood.

Manifestation: When an entity such as a ghost tries to make itself known to the living and creates a visible form, or partially visible form.

Materialization: The act of forming a shape in the air that is recognizable.

Medium: A psychic who regularly talks to the spirit world. Often someone who is clairaudient, clairsentient, and clairvoyant. Mediums may conduct séances.

Mist: Possibly related to an entity attempting to manifest itself, a visible mist or fog–like formation, usually indoors, that is unexplainable.

Motor Automatism: Spirit control over a person's body, as in automatic writing.

Dear Death Experience or NDE: An experience reported by people who have been clinically dead and revived, then report encounters with spirits, angels, dead relatives and sometimes a life review and out of the body experience. Some people who have had an NDE become intuitive, psychic, or more empathic. Some even have a complete personality change. Most no longer fear death.

Night Vision: Infrared (**IR**) radiation is electromagnetic radiation whose wavelength is longer than that of visible light. The name means "below red" (from the Latin *infra*, "below"), red being the color of visible light with the longest wavelength. Infrared radiation has wavelengths between about 750 nm. Infrared is used in night vision equipment and is used when there is insufficient visible light to see normally.

Orb: An anomalous object, usually an independent light source that does not illuminate other objects and is believed to be spirits of the dead or other beings. Orbs typically range in size from the size of a pea to three feet in diameter and have been associated with haunting and portals. Orbs sometimes are visible to the naked eye, but appear more often on video or still photos. Orbs can change shapes, size, and can contain faces or geometric patterns. Orbs are still not fully understood by the paranormal community.

Ouija Board: A board used to communicate with spirits. A planchette is used by two people who lightly touch it to allow the spirit to spell out words or point to yes or no answers. Often the use of a Ouija board by inexperienced persons can lead to opening communication with a negative entity rather than the desired spirit.

Out-of-body Experience or OBE: A sensation or experience in which ones self or spirit travels to a different location than their physical body. OBE's are associated with involuntary astral projection.

Paranormal: Events that cannot be explained by conventional means and are out of the range of normal everyday occurrences or current scientific knowledge.

Parapsychology: The scientific study of paranormal phenomena coined by J.B Rhine.

Phantom or Ghost: Something that is seen, heard, or sensed, but has no physical reality. Also called a phantasm.

Poltergeist: Associated with physical activity such as thrown objects, breaking dishes, fire starting, stone throwing, lifting objects, etc. and may be related to a real "noisy" spirit or an adolescent female in the house who generates excess energy unconsciously. Literally means "Noisy Spirit."

Portal: In theory, an opening to another dimension or time.

Possession: When a person's body is apparently taken over by another personality or entity. Associated with mediumship and demonic possession.

Psychic: Someone who has one or more abilities to see, hear, or sense out of the normal range of most people- this ability is often called extra-sensory perception or ESP for short

Psychokinesis (PK): or Telekinesis from the Greek "kinesis", meaning motion. The influence of the mind on physical items, i.e. moving or bending objects.

Psychometry: The ability to obtain knowledge by holding a physical object owned by a person.

Radio Voice Phenomenon or RVP: Receiving the voice of a deceased human being through a regular radio (usually AM).

Remote Viewer: Someone who projects their consciousness to another location, looks around, and describes or draws what they see at that location. Some remote viewers are very accurate, and some have the ability to look into the past or future when remote viewing.

Retrocognition: Paranormal knowledge of past events.

Séance: A gathering of people who attempt to receive messages from ghosts or spirits, or to listen to a spirit medium speak with or relay messages from spirits. Should be facilitated by an experienced medium.

Shadow person: (or entity) A term used to describe dark, usually human-like menacing forms. A phenomena that is not completely understood.

Shape-Shifting: The ability to assume the form of another person, animal or other entity.

Simulacra: The seeing of faces, figures, and images in everyday objects such as walls, rocks, carpet, foliage, etc.

Sleep Paralysis: A state between sleep and awake, where a person is unable to move.

Speaking in Tongues: Unintelligible or unknown speech uttered in a trance state.

Specter: A ghostly apparition or phantom.

Spirit: The essence of a human being, animal, or other living thing. Spirits maintain their previous life personality (in my experience).

Spiritualism: The belief system that the dead are able to communicate with the living, through and intermediary or medium.

Spontaneous Human Combustion: Rare cases where a badly burned body is found with little or no damage to surrounding structures, suspected to originate inside the body of the victim.

Stigmata: The appearance of unexplained marks or open wounds on the body corresponding to the location to the crucifixion wounds of Christ in the feet, hands, or wrists. Usually only experienced by very devout Catholics.

Succubus: A demon in female form who lies with men while they are sleeping.

Subject: A person who is being studied or investigated.

Supernatural: Opposite of natural—phenomena having to do with divine or demonic intervention or experience.

Table-Tilting or Table-Tipping: Unexplained movement of a table, usually during a séance where a group of people join hands or touch fingers around the table.

Target: The objet or vent which a subject attempts to perceive, usually having to do with ESP testing.

Telekinesis: The ability to move or distort objects by using the mind to project energy. i.e. bending spoons using the mind.

Telepathy: Communication via extra-sensory-perception rather than the five senses. Awareness of another person's experience. Often used in ghost hunting to communicate with deceased persons.

Third Eye: The area between the eyes on the forehead that is the location used as a means of communication by psychics or clairvoyants. This area will often buzz or tingle when the psychic is using it. Some psychics mentally "turn the third eye on" or activate it consciously, before sending their consciousness out to view anything.

Thought Form: An apparition of a being or object produced solely by the power of the human mind or collectively as a group.

Time Imprint: (also known as an Imprint or Residual Haunting) Similar to watching a movie, a time imprint is the energy left behind by activity, usually repeated over and over again in a specific location. There is no ghost or spirit, just the energy of the person or objects. A time imprint will not interact with people.

Trance: An altered state of consciousness, self-induced or induced by a hypnotist in order to access the subconscious mind and communicate with entities such as spirits, or guides.

Transpersonal Psychology: The study of practices and believes that suggest that the sense of self can extend beyond our physical reality.

Tree Spirit: Spirits who live inside of trees. May have been human in previous lifetimes and will often manifest their likeness in the bark or knots in the tree. Tree spirits can communicate telepathically with humans.

Tree Sprite: A Non-human entity or elemental who help trees grow, flower, leaf, grow limbs, and go dormant. Usually visible as tiny bright white/blue orbs which are in constant movement around trees. Tree sprites can communicate telepathically with humans, and may be visible to some psychics or with night vision equipment. There are usually a great number of tree sprites around trees.

Unidentified Flying Object (UFO): Unexplained objects in the sky often associated with alien visitation or visitation from people from the future. Also associated with Underwater Submerged Objects (USO).

Veridical dream: A dream that corresponds to events that are unknown to the dreamer, but later confirmed by facts and events.

Vortex: In theory—a portal or doorway to other dimensions, possibly linked to Ley Lines and electromagnetic fields of the earth. Often appears as a funnel or rope-like tube, possibly a wormhole in time-space.

White Noise: Use of a television turned to a channel with no programming, or a radio tuned to a frequency without programming in order to hear or see ghosts. White noise CDs are also available. It is thought that ghosts are able to communicate more easily while white noise is played. Fans can also produce white noise.

Worm Hole: A theoretical entity or topological feature allowed by Einstein's theory of general relativity in which space/time curvature connects two distant locations or times, allowing for a "shortcut" through space/time.

Bibliography

Books

Barton, John, and John Muddiman, eds. "The Oxford Bible Commentary." New York: Oxford University Press, 2001.

Bord, Janet, "Fairies: Real Encounters With Little People, Mass Market Paperback

Brooks, Claire M. "A Cultivator's View of Reincarnation Cases in Western Medical Research." Reincarnation Cases 2003. 20 August 2004 www.pureinsight.org/pi/articles/2002/9/2/213p.html.

Cannon, Timothy L. and Whitmore, Nancy F. "Ghosts & Legends of Frederick County"

Friedman, Stanton and Marden, Kathleen, "Science Was Wrong" New Page Books 2010

Haining, Peter. "The Mammoth book of Haunted House Stories" 2005

Hollis, Heidi. "*The Secret War: The Heavens Speak of the Battle.*" Author House, 2001. *www.shadows.ufo2u.com.*

Offutt, Jason. "Haunted Missouri: A Ghostly Guide to the Show-Me State's Most Spirited Spots." Truman University Press 2007

Offutt, Jason. "Darkness Walks: The Shadow People Among Us" Anomalist Books 2009

Kirk, Robert, "The Secret Common-Wealth, edited with a commentary by Stewart Sanderson, D.S. Brewer, Suffolk, and Rowman and Littlefield, N.J., 1976

Riccio, Delores. "Haunted Houses U.S.A." 1989

Taylor, Troy. "Spirits of the Civil War." 1999

Van Praagh, James. "Ghost Among Us. Uncovering the Truth About the Other Side" Harper One, May 13, 2008.

Winkowski, Mary Ann, "When Ghosts Speak: Understanding the World of Earthbound spirits" Mass Market Paperback, Oct. 1, 2009

Eason, Cassandra. "The Modern-Day Druidess." Citadel, 2004

Knight, Sirona. "Fairy Magick." New Page books, 2003

Websites

Wikipedia: en.wikipedia.org/wiki/Paranormal.

Yahoo Dictionary: www.yahoo.com.

Paranormal news: www.paranormalnews.com.

Paranormal Dictionary: www.studiesoftheparanormal.com/paranormaldictionary.html

The Mystica website. themystica.com/mystica/articles/p/poltergeist.html.

Mystical Blaze: www.mysticalblaze.com

Frederic Gimino, the Free Psychic network, www.freepsychicnetwork.com

Haunted America Tours, www.hauntedamericatours.com

From the Shadows: from-the-shadows.blogspot.com

The Faery-Faith Network: www.faeryfaith.org

Fairy Source: www.fairysource.com

Shadow People—the Psychic Detective: the-psychic-detective.com/shadow-People.htm

Demonology: www.djmcadam.com/demons.htm

www. Ask.com

The Certified Haunted House

Some hotel and restaurant owners want proof that their site is haunted in order to use for promotional purposes. When we certify that a place as haunted, we go through all of the procedures mentioned in this book and do our own investigation on site. We may return several times to the same place. If we find several anomalous things about a location that cannot be explained any other way, we may issue a Certified Haunted Location certificate or plaque. For more information please visit www.margiekay.com.

About the Author

Margie Kay is a native of Kansas City and lives in Independence, Missouri with her husband, Gene. Kay has a B.A. in Business Administration, and an M.A. in Technical Writing. She is a nationally-known speaker, has written numerous articles for magazines and newspapers, and is the author of over a dozen books on various topics. She is the publisher of Un-X News Magazine.

Kay was host of QUEST radio show on KCXL in Kansas City for five years, and has been a guest on many national radio and television programs. She now hosts Un-X News Radio on KGRA at www.kgraradio.com.

Margie's interest in the paranormal began at a very early age. She showed psychic abilities before the age of five, and began to see spirits at the age of 11. Kay's natural abilities to see through objects and people, predict events, and do remote viewing of real-time or the past have astounded many. She has the special gift of medical diagnosis and viewing the interior of bodies to see where problem areas are. Kay often does on-the-spot readings at conferences so the entire audience can see the results.

Kay's abilities have led to solving many missing person cases and homicides. Law enforcement and private investigators from all over the world have called her to help with difficult and unsolved cases. The QUEST Investigation Group, which includes her two psychic daughters and other professionals, have worked together to help solve crimes and do haunted location investigations and certifications nationwide.

Margie is the director of the annual Paracon conference in Kansas City, Missouri where internationally known researchers share their experiences and research. Margie is available for speaking engagements. Visit www.margiekay.com for more information.

Also by Margie Kay

Un-X News Magazine, Quarterly (2011-present)
Haunted Independence (2010)
The Ghost Hunter's Field Guide (2010)
Color Therapy Wall Chart (1999)
Handbook for Goddesses (1997)

For more about Margie Kay, including upcoming books and documentaries, visit www.MargieKay.com

"I heard that kind of a sound that a ghost makes when it wants to tell about something that's on its mind and can't make itself understood, and so can't rest easy in its grave, and has to go about that way every night grieving."

Mark Twain

Index

A

abductees, 36
abilities, 7-8, 36, 42, 46-47, 51, 104, 228, 237, 246
ability, 14, 36, 47, 50, 52, 54-55, 89-90, 106, 171, 230, 237-239
active, 9, 34, 59, 147, 159, 168, 203-204, 220-221
Adam, 193-194, 217
Adams, 191-194, 214, 218
adept, 43
Administration, 246
adolescent, 236
adult, 111, 148
adults, 14, 39, 92, 108, 134, 181, 185
aetv, 225-226
afraid, 7, 22, 28, 92, 109, 131-132, 146, 170, 174
African, 174
afterlife, 20
Agate, 101-102
age, 7-9, 20, 30, 109, 131, 173, 179, 192, 246
Agency, 210
Agent, 229
agents, 217
ages, 20, 22, 108
air, 37, 60, 62, 88, 91, 109, 111, 113-114, 128, 135-136, 160, 173, 192, 201, 231, 234
airplane, 150
Airs, 225
Akashic, 35, 229
Al, 185, 213-214
Alabama, 212, 224
Alamo, 209, 220
alarm, 87, 152, 154, 160, 194
alarmed, 109
Alaska, 224
alaskaparanormal, 224
Albert, 36
Alcatraz, 213
alcatraz, 213
Alcohol, 45
alcohol, 45
Alexander, 218
Alfred, 234
Alice, 16, 192
alien, 36-37, 113, 122, 240
Aliens, 5, 23, 35-36, 114
aliens, 11, 23, 30, 35-37, 122
alignments, 234
Alnwick, 216
Alpha, 42
altered, 240
aluminum, 165
Amber, 102
Ambient, 93
ambient, 58
ambulance, 155
America, 199, 202, 205, 208, 243
American, 17, 26-27, 133, 174, 213
Americans, 26, 81, 122
Amulet, 229
analytical, 51, 54
ancestors, 14-15, 22, 140

Index

Ancestry, 90, 226
ancient, 33, 232, 234
Andrew, 202
Andulasite, 101
angel, 76
angels, 11, 30, 53, 235
Animals, 88
animals, 88, 114, 176
Ann, 107, 243
Anna, 136, 192
Anne, 136-137, 192, 214
Annette, 225
Annie, 77, 126, 136
anomalies, 78, 162
Anomalist, 242
Anomalous, 229
anomalous, 5, 57-58, 72, 76, 189-190, 235, 245
Anomaly, 224
anomalyradio, 224
antibiotics, 15
Antietam, 209
antiquaries, 216
Antonio, 209, 220
Apparition, 229, 231, 233
apparition, 16, 33, 41, 77-78, 82-84, 118, 127-129, 149, 155, 161, 164-165, 178, 183, 187, 199-200, 204-207, 212, 217, 231, 233, 238, 240
Apparitions, 5, 33, 212-213
apparitions, 11, 14, 33, 36, 50, 72, 121, 129, 135, 158, 198-199, 201, 208-211, 219-220, 222
apples, 206
April, 176
Aquamarine, 102
AR, 204, 208
arch, 67
archive, 226
Archives, 226
archives, 171, 224, 226
archivesearch, 226
Arizona, 219
Arkadelphia, 212
Arkansas, 31, 99, 180, 204, 212
arm, 15, 100, 118, 146, 148, 158, 174, 219
armory, 214
arms, 183, 191
Armstrong, 184
Army, 210
arrival, 27, 29, 97, 121, 124, 164, 186, 203
arrived, 10, 110, 129, 132, 138, 155, 186, 192
arrives, 20
arriving, 97, 181
arthritis, 44
article, 83
articles, 90, 168, 226, 242-243, 246
artifacts, 194
artificial, 45
Artistic, 34
artistic, 54
Astral, 21, 229-230
astral, 12, 21, 23, 28, 37, 229-230, 236
Asylum, 200
Atlantic, 217, 225
atoms, 30
attacked, 192, 216
attract, 168
attraction, 193, 221-222
audible, 27, 86, 101, 110, 232
Audio, 93
audio, 62, 91, 93, 154, 224
auditorium, 213
Audubon, 205
August, 15, 19, 78, 114, 118, 152, 202, 242
Aura, 230
aura, 12, 102, 230, 234
auras, 46, 230
Automatic, 230
automatic, 23, 235
Automatism, 230, 235
Autoscopy, 230
Ax, 198
axe, 198, 202

B

baby, 15, 84, 115, 220
bachelor, 7
Bachelors, 199
bachelorsgrove, 199
bacteria, 60
Ball, 5, 30, 230
ball, 20, 23, 27, 29-31, 50, 64, 90-91, 116, 201, 230
ballroom, 204
balls, 21, 29-30, 79, 199
band, 104-105
banging, 8, 26, 36-37, 88, 115-116, 123-124, 181
banish, 233

Index

Banshee, 230
bar, 186, 188, 190, 221
bark, 240
barking, 117
Barnhart, 152, 154-155
Barry, 225
Barton, 242
basement, 108-109, 111, 138, 145, 154, 186-187
bass, 105
bathroom, 8, 108, 121, 142, 148, 181
bathtub, 203
bats, 88
batteries, 23, 33, 59, 63
battery, 136-137
Battle, 242
battle, 123, 125, 208-209, 211, 220
Battlefield, 208-209, 211
battlefield, 208-209, 211
Battlefields, 208
battlegrounds, 82
battles, 216
Bay, 126, 191
BE, 69
Be, 43, 58-61, 64, 82-83, 91, 99, 222
be, 2, 9, 11-15, 20-26, 28-31, 33-39, 41-44, 46, 48-53, 55, 57-68, 71, 78-83, 87-92, 96-98, 101, 104-106, 109, 111-116, 118-120, 122, 124-125, 127-128, 131-132, 135-136, 143-145, 147, 149-150, 152, 156, 158-164, 170-171, 177, 179-182, 185, 187-189, 191, 193, 197-201, 203, 205-206, 208-210, 212, 216, 218-220, 222, 226, 230-237, 240, 245
Beach, 217
beam, 30
beams, 30
Becket, 214
Bed, 201-202
bed, 39, 42, 87, 105, 115, 117, 121, 123, 146, 148-149, 170-171, 186, 193, 202
bedrock, 185
bedroom, 9, 27, 38, 108, 115-117, 121, 123, 126, 132, 147-150, 172, 175, 188-189, 193, 202, 212, 218
being, 25-26, 30, 37-38, 49, 54, 78, 87, 96, 116, 125, 131, 133, 140, 145-146, 149, 155, 168-169, 181, 184, 187, 191-192, 206, 216, 218, 225, 230, 233, 235, 237-240
beings, 11-12, 20, 25, 28, 37-39, 48, 104, 106, 112, 114-115, 117, 150, 232, 235
belief, 238
believe, 9, 11-12, 14, 28-29, 31, 38-39, 44-45, 48, 51, 68, 77, 87, 104, 117, 128, 132, 135-136, 145, 148, 158-159, 174, 192, 215, 229
believed, 15, 33, 192, 231, 235
believes, 87, 240
Bell, 214-215, 224
bell, 143, 158-159
Bells, 84
bellwitchcave, 214
benevolent, 191
benign, 173
Bess, 157, 198
Beta, 42, 211
beta, 42
Betsy, 203
Bettie, 131-132
Betty, 49
beyond, 49, 134, 240
Bible, 242
Bibliography, 6, 242
Bighorn, 209
Bill, 184-185, 191, 194-195
bill, 192
Binoculars, 59, 227
Birch, 117
Bishop, 206, 225
bizarre, 104-105, 116
Black, 98, 101-102, 130-131, 184, 194, 212, 216, 233
black, 9, 16, 25, 27, 37-38, 43, 50, 54, 61, 63, 98, 101, 105, 113, 121, 123, 129-131, 134, 143, 149-150, 160-161, 171, 218-219
blacker, 37-38
Blair, 220
Blaze, 243
blocktalkradio, 224
blogspot, 243
Blood, 84
blood, 15, 221
bloodiest, 208-209
bloody, 219
blowing, 52, 105
BLT, 30
bltresearch, 30
Blue, 101-102
blue, 90, 171, 183, 209, 217, 240
Board, 236
board, 54, 96, 236
Bobby, 207
bodies, 12, 37, 182, 215, 230, 246
Boleyn, 214

Bolton, 204
book, 2, 4, 8, 10-11, 28-29, 35, 39, 45, 48, 53-55, 76, 82-83, 144, 149, 169, 190, 218, 221, 242, 245, 247
Books, 242, 247
books, 7, 45, 51, 61, 158, 165, 226, 243, 246
bookshelves, 159
boomtown, 219
Boonville, 78
Bordon, 202
bordon, 202
Bowie, 209
boxes, 58, 87, 153
Boyd, 160
boys, 115-116, 131-132
Brad, 225
Bradford, 201
brain, 42, 87
brainwaves, 42
brass, 66
Brethwaite, 113, 138, 159, 161, 168
Brewer, 242
brick, 57, 136, 164, 203
bricked, 217
bricks, 163
bridge, 144, 220
bridges, 82
Bridget, 206
Britain, 217
Britannica, 7
British, 177
Broadcasting, 223
broadcasts, 226
Brooks, 242
Brothel, 194
brothels, 185, 194
brother, 7, 16-17, 77, 105, 131, 170, 179-182
brothers, 77
Buell, 225
Building, 156, 218
building, 10, 38, 83, 88, 102, 123, 146, 151-153, 157-158, 163, 173, 175-177, 187, 194, 198, 203, 206
buildings, 14, 26, 36, 51, 60, 81-82, 152, 211, 219
Built, 164, 205, 207-208, 217
bulldozers, 99
Bullock, 184-191, 203
Bulls, 101
Bureau, 210
burglar, 110
Burial, 102
burial, 26, 82, 199
buried, 77, 87, 107, 134, 136, 181, 185, 191, 219
Burke, 215
Burkittsville, 220-221
burned, 131, 133, 136, 146, 163, 238
Burning, 84
burning, 125, 140
bus, 220
Business, 246
business, 7, 52, 79, 86, 96, 108, 112-114, 122, 134, 185
businesses, 157, 185, 215
Butler, 36

C

cabin, 124, 146
cabinet, 52, 109, 124, 160, 171
cabinets, 110, 124
cabins, 135
Calamity, 185, 191
Calhoun, 169
California, 192, 198-199, 213, 217
camcorder, 58
camcorders, 33
Camera, 59, 63, 231
camera, 58-59, 63-64, 71, 93-94, 118, 120, 129, 136, 141, 152, 154-155, 158-159, 188-190, 197, 203, 219, 231
Cameras, 5, 58, 227
cameras, 33, 57-59, 71-72, 76, 94, 162, 222, 227, 231
cancer, 87, 192
candle, 105
Cannon, 53, 242
cannon, 209, 211
Canoe, 214
Canon, 227
Capone, 213-214
capsized, 220
captains, 206
capture, 10, 41, 60, 190, 221, 231
captured, 62, 190, 202, 208, 211
Carbon, 109
carbon, 140
carcinogenic, 89
card, 8, 47, 58-59

Cards, 47-48
cards, 8, 47
Caretakers, 191
caretakers, 191
Caribbean, 82
Carnelian, 101
Carpathian, 215
carpenters, 198
Carrollton, 17
cars, 220
Casino, 191, 194
Cassandra, 243
Cassie, 175
Castle, 215-216
castle, 216-217
Cat, 218
cat, 7-8, 113, 121, 132, 147, 170, 204, 218
Catacombs, 215, 221
catacombs, 215
catastrophes, 53
Catherine, 214
Catholics, 239
catle, 217
cats, 115
Cave, 214, 220
cave, 215, 220
caves, 33
Cayce, 8
CD, 42-44, 62, 93, 227, 241
ceiling, 9, 140-141, 150, 153
ceilings, 87
Cell, 93
cell, 46, 58, 63, 82, 87, 174-175
cellar, 219
cells, 46, 173-174
Cemeteries, 199
cemeteries, 200
Cemetery, 78, 107, 127, 134, 191, 199-200
cemetery, 78, 127-130, 191, 193, 199-200, 209
chalcedony, 101-102
chamber, 67
chambers, 67
Channeling, 230
chanting, 210
chapel, 163, 178
Charleston, 212
chasekloetzke, 223
Chattanooga, 209
Chicago, 199, 212, 219, 226
Chickamauga, 209
chill, 38
chilling, 171
Chillingham, 216
chillingham, 217
chills, 27, 85, 207
chimney, 61, 75, 88, 140, 147, 149-150, 161-164, 166-169, 177
Chimneys, 6, 161, 163
chimneys, 88, 149, 161-163, 166-168, 232
Chloe, 205
Chris, 113, 138, 140, 159, 161, 168
Christ, 238
Christian, 28
Christine, 4, 247
Chronicles, 200
Church, 134, 209
church, 38, 134
churches, 82
Circle, 47
circle, 8, 30, 97
circles, 30, 161
circuitry, 88
Citadel, 243
Clairaudience, 52
clairaudience, 8, 49, 233
Clairaudient, 231
clairaudient, 62, 235
Claire, 242
Clairsentience, 49
clairsentience, 8, 49, 233
Clairsentient, 231
clairsentient, 62, 235
Clairvoyance, 50
clairvoyance, 8, 49, 233
Clairvoyant, 231
clairvoyant, 8, 50, 62, 235
clairvoyants, 229-230, 234, 239
Clapp, 219
Clark, 186, 203, 210, 213, 219-220
Claudia, 183
clay, 5, 99
cleanse, 99-101
cleansed, 98, 101
Cleansing, 99
cleansing, 100
Clear, 43, 66
clear, 11, 34, 41, 43, 49-50, 62, 65-66, 75, 78-79, 98, 100-101, 158
cleared, 134
Clinton, 157

cloak, 37
Cloud, 4, 17
clouds, 76, 93
CO, 202
coal, 163
Coast, 223-224
coasttocoastam, 224
cobra, 186, 203
cocoon, 97
coexist, 30
coffins, 191
Colbert, 4
Coleman, 99, 207
Coliseum, 216
College, 169, 211-212
college, 212
Colonel, 184
colonel, 163
Colonial, 81
Colorado, 16, 202, 212
Columbia, 211
combination, 41, 106
Confederate, 81, 145, 175, 211, 213
confederate, 125, 199
Congress, 218
Conqueror, 214
conscious, 51, 230, 232
consciously, 239
Consciousness, 5, 44, 72
consciousness, 23-24, 30, 41-42, 45, 51, 229, 237, 239-240
Constitution, 218
cosmic, 12
Costner, 185
Courthouse, 221
courthouses, 82
CPU, 61
craft, 36-37
crash, 93, 115
crashing, 124
Creek, 127, 180-181, 185, 191
creek, 134
Crescent, 204
crescent, 204
Crockett, 209
Crop, 30
crop, 30
cross, 8, 22, 68, 78, 232
crossing, 143-144, 199
crossings, 217
Crossroads, 225
crossroadsparanormal, 225
Crow, 210
Crystal, 99-100
crystal, 31, 66, 90, 98-101
Crystals, 5, 63, 98-100
crystals, 98-100
Curacao, 217
curiosity, 161
Cutts, 223

D

Dakota, 184
damper, 88-89
Dan, 179-180
Dark, 100, 131
dark, 9, 34-35, 37-38, 63, 82-83, 111, 117, 123-124, 128-133, 138, 154, 156, 158, 161, 170, 174, 192, 200, 203, 209, 222, 233, 238
darken, 58
darkessradio, 224
Darkness, 224, 242
darkness, 59
David, 28, 201, 224
davidickebooks, 28
Davy, 209
DC, 218
Dead, 1-4, 6, 8, 10, 12, 14, 16, 18, 20, 22, 24, 26, 28, 30, 32, 34, 36, 38, 40, 42, 44, 46, 48, 50, 52, 54, 56, 58, 60, 62, 64, 66, 68, 70, 72, 74, 76, 78, 80, 82, 84, 86, 88, 90, 92, 94, 96, 98, 100, 102, 104, 106, 108, 110, 112, 114, 116, 118, 120, 122, 124, 126, 128, 130, 132, 134, 136, 138, 140, 142, 144, 146, 148, 150, 152, 154, 156, 158, 160, 162, 164, 166, 168, 170, 172, 174, 176, 178, 180, 182, 184, 186, 188, 190, 192, 194, 196, 198, 200, 202, 204, 206, 208, 210, 212, 214, 216, 218, 220, 222, 224, 226, 228, 230, 232, 234, 236, 238, 240, 242, 244, 246, 248
dead, 12, 16, 19, 27, 53, 96, 110, 116, 121, 135, 148-149, 177, 198, 205, 215-216, 231, 235, 238
deadly, 222
Deadwood, 184-186, 191, 193-195, 203
deadwood, 195

■ Index

deceased, 11, 16, 29, 37, 39, 53, 84, 90, 160, 181, 183, 233, 237, 239
DeHaven, 78
Deimer, 211
Déjà, 21, 54, 231
Delores, 243
Deloris, 53
DeMerit, 201
Demon, 218, 231
demon, 28, 102, 231, 234, 239
demonic, 29, 231, 237, 239
demonologist, 29
demonologists, 28
Demonology, 244
Demons, 5, 28
demons, 28-29, 244
Denfert, 215
Dennis, 31-32
Denver, 212
Depot, 144
Device, 64
devices, 91, 142
devil, 28, 231
devilish, 28
devout, 239
diameter, 27, 32, 61, 101, 130, 150, 235
Dictionary, 243
Dicus, 78, 138-139
die, 24, 126
died, 15, 52-53, 62, 81-82, 106, 109, 124, 126, 154, 156, 158, 165, 182-183, 186, 192-193, 198, 203, 205, 209, 211-212, 214, 219-221
Diego, 199
dies, 23-24, 35
dimension, 11-12, 37, 39, 41, 53, 112, 114, 150, 237
dimensional, 113-114, 170, 230
dimensions, 12, 24, 37, 112, 161, 166, 241
dimes, 221
dining, 118, 123, 148, 154, 205
dinner, 202
Direct, 232
direct, 184
director, 177, 224, 246
disappear, 36, 121, 150, 158, 207, 222, 229
disappearance, 179
disappeared, 16, 31, 39, 84, 86, 109, 113-114, 131, 133-134, 140, 143, 154, 170, 192
disappearing, 33
disappears, 206
disappointed, 186, 203
disembodied, 39, 158, 201, 215
disruptive, 45
District, 208
disturbed, 42, 133
disturbing, 9, 163
divine, 239
divining, 65
Dobyns, 78
Doctor, 208
doctor, 9, 170, 208, 212
doctors, 15
documentary, 247
documented, 199
Dolan, 223
Don, 44-45, 48, 55, 62, 67, 96, 208, 211
Door, 84, 194
door, 31, 110-111, 115-116, 118, 121, 130-131, 140, 148, 152, 158-159, 164, 171, 189, 192
doors, 8-9, 27, 46, 60, 96, 110, 114, 117, 124, 130, 153, 158, 171, 204
doorway, 26, 115, 160, 241
Doppelganger, 232
dormant, 34, 240
dormer, 108
dormitories, 211
double, 59, 66, 100
Doug, 225
Dowse, 5, 60, 65
dowse, 65, 67, 228
dowsed, 180
dowser, 68
dowsers, 67-68
Dowsing, 5, 45, 60, 65, 67-69, 100, 232
dowsing, 5, 45, 48, 54, 60, 65-68, 97, 155, 228, 234
Dracula, 215
Draft, 167, 169, 232
draft, 166-169, 177, 232
Dreamland, 224
dreams, 21, 181
Druidess, 243
Drury, 169
Duke, 47
dungeons, 216-217

E

Earthbound, 232, 243
earthly, 24
earthquakes, 53
easternstate, 214
Eastland, 220
Ectoplasm, 232
Ed, 104, 225
Eddie, 224
Edgar, 8
Edinburgh, 215-216
edinburghcastle, 216
eerie, 38
Eighth, 178
Einstein, 241
Electrical, 87
Electro, 87
electro, 87
Electromagnetic, 13
electromagnetic, 12, 46, 58, 87, 232, 235, 241
Electronic, 60, 232
electrons, 30
elemental, 240
Elementals, 232
elementals, 41, 89
Elizabeth, 218
Ellis, 211
elves, 232
Emerald, 247
EMF, 5, 58, 63, 87-88, 91, 94, 138, 142, 147, 159, 228, 232-233
EMFs, 87
Emmitsburg, 212
empathic, 235
encounter, 8, 25, 38, 100, 145, 213, 231
encountered, 89, 214, 219
Encounters, 5, 103, 127, 134, 163, 242
encounters, 11, 36, 38, 84, 186, 211, 235
Energy, 234
energy, 7, 12, 23, 25, 28, 30, 33-35, 38-39, 46, 59, 65, 68, 79, 96, 98, 100-102, 105, 111, 122, 132-133, 137, 155, 168, 174, 203, 230, 234, 236, 239-240
England, 126, 176, 216
English, 126
Entities, 5, 25, 103
entities, 9-11, 13, 23, 25, 28, 36, 45, 104, 112, 114, 121-122, 133, 165, 209, 233, 240
Entity, 233
entity, 25-27, 29, 31, 37-39, 98, 104, 124, 133, 155, 230-231, 234-238, 240-241
EOC, 227
eocinstitute, 227
Equipment, 93, 227
equipment, 5, 41, 57, 60, 91-94, 138, 222, 233, 235, 240
esoteric, 104
ESP, 8, 47, 233, 237, 239
essence, 11, 21, 65-66, 238
Estes, 202
Eternal, 247
ethereal, 232
Eureka, 204
Europe, 82
Evidence, 83
evidence, 10, 14, 28, 35, 37, 39, 54-55, 57, 59, 71, 88-90, 92-93, 111
evidenced, 15
Evil, 102
evil, 28-29, 102, 104, 106, 231
EVP, 60, 101
EVPs, 202, 222
Exorcism, 233
Exorcist, 105
exorcists, 28
Extrasensory, 233
Eye, 101-102, 223, 239
eye, 18, 29, 33, 38, 41, 50-51, 58-59, 73-74, 79, 81, 89, 104, 109, 114, 122, 129, 162, 183, 189, 204, 231-232, 236, 239

F

Faery, 244
faeryfaith, 244
Fairies, 5, 242
fairies, 11, 30, 89, 232
Fairmont, 191
Fairmount, 145, 213-214
Fairy, 79, 243-244
fairy, 137
fairysource, 244

FBI, 182
Fear, 85
fear, 24, 27, 37, 39, 96, 104-106, 117, 132-133, 235
fearful, 165
fears, 7, 28-29
Feickert, 202
Feliciana, 205
Fever, 192
Field, 1-3, 5, 7, 9, 11, 13, 15, 17, 19, 21, 23, 25, 27, 29-31, 33, 35, 37, 39, 41, 43, 45, 47, 49, 51, 53, 55, 57, 59, 61, 63, 65, 67, 69, 71, 73, 75, 77, 79, 81, 83, 85, 87, 89, 91, 93, 95, 97, 99, 101, 103, 105, 107, 109, 111, 113, 115, 117, 119, 121, 123, 125, 127, 129, 131, 133, 135, 137, 139, 141, 143, 145, 147, 149, 151, 153, 155, 157, 159, 161, 163, 165, 167, 169, 171, 173, 175, 177, 179, 181, 183, 185, 187, 189, 191, 193, 195, 197, 199, 201, 203, 205, 207, 209, 211, 213, 215, 217, 219, 221, 223, 225, 227, 229, 231, 233, 235, 237, 239, 241, 243, 245, 247
field, 10, 12, 30, 35, 57, 87-88, 93, 101, 230
Fifth, 37
film, 26, 30, 33, 36, 41, 72, 90, 92, 106, 129, 142, 162-163, 177, 189, 198, 202, 211, 247
filmed, 177
filming, 62, 129
fire, 17, 72, 125, 135, 163-165, 169, 202, 215, 236
fireplace, 138, 147, 158, 162-165, 168-169, 177, 194
fireplaces, 161-163, 166
fires, 125, 135, 219
Fitzgerald, 223
Five, 211
five, 7, 16, 27, 47, 49, 109, 129-130, 162, 207, 220, 233, 239, 246
Fivepointed, 47
flame, 125, 165
flashlight, 82
Flashlights, 63
Flora, 203
Florida, 82
flower, 240
Flowers, 84
flowers, 118
Floyd, 217
flue, 109, 165, 168
Fluorite, 102
Fog, 5, 31-33, 84
fog, 31-33, 36, 50, 72, 74, 79, 129, 142, 148-149, 162, 210, 235
forensics, 10
Forest, 219
Fort, 163-165, 209-210
fossil, 194
France, 215
Francisco, 213
Francisville, 201, 205
Frank, 19, 77, 107, 136, 138, 147, 160, 173-174, 199, 213, 217
Franklin, 192, 194
Franklins, 192
Fred, 163, 203, 212, 219
Frederic, 243
Frederick, 200, 242
Free, 228, 243
free, 19, 23, 30, 217, 226
freely, 67
freepsychicnetwork, 243
freezer, 49
freight, 217
frequency, 41, 45, 62, 123, 241
frequent, 48, 160
Friedman, 37, 242

G

Gables, 219
Gallows, 219
Gambling, 194
gambling, 185
Gamma, 13, 211
Garfield, 138, 218
Gateway, 1-3, 6, 8, 10, 12, 14, 16, 18, 20, 22, 24, 26, 28, 30, 32, 34, 36, 38, 40, 42, 44, 46, 48, 50, 52, 54, 56, 58, 60, 62, 64, 66, 68, 70, 72, 74, 76, 78, 80, 82, 84, 86, 88, 90, 92, 94, 96, 98, 100, 102, 104, 106, 108, 110, 112, 114, 116, 118, 120, 122, 124, 126, 128, 130, 132, 134, 136, 138, 140, 142, 144, 146, 148, 150, 152, 154, 156, 158, 160, 162, 164, 166, 168, 170, 172, 174, 176, 178, 180, 182, 184, 186, 188, 190, 192, 194, 196, 198, 200, 202, 204, 206, 208, 210, 212, 214, 216, 218, 220, 222, 224, 226, 228, 230, 232, 234, 236, 238, 240, 242, 244, 246, 248
gathering, 150, 237
Gauss, 87-88
Gaussmeter, 233

Gene, 109, 187, 195, 225, 246
Genealogy, 226
geometric, 236
George, 135, 154, 183-184, 198, 205, 223
Georgia, 205, 209
German, 221
Germantown, 210
GESP, 233
Gettysburg, 208
Ghost, 1-3, 5-7, 9-11, 13, 15, 17, 19, 21, 23, 25, 27, 29, 31, 33, 35, 37, 39, 41, 43, 45, 47, 49, 51, 53, 55, 57, 59, 61, 63, 65, 67, 69, 71, 73, 75, 77, 79, 81, 83, 85, 87, 89, 91, 93, 95, 97, 99, 101, 103, 105, 107, 109, 111, 113, 115, 117, 119, 121, 123, 125, 127, 129, 131, 133, 135, 137, 139, 141, 143, 145, 147, 149, 151, 153, 155, 157, 159, 161, 163, 165, 167, 169, 171, 173, 175, 177, 179, 181, 183, 185, 187, 189, 191, 193, 195, 197, 199, 201, 203, 205, 207, 209, 211, 213, 215, 217, 219, 221, 223, 225-229, 231, 233, 235-237, 239, 241, 243, 245, 247
ghost, 10, 14, 18, 25-26, 28-29, 33, 36, 39, 41, 44, 49, 53-54, 57-60, 62-65, 67-68, 71-73, 76, 79, 81-83, 85-93, 96-98, 106-107, 110, 116, 121, 125-129, 134-136, 138, 140, 143-145, 152-153, 155-156, 159, 161, 163-166, 168, 170-172, 174-176, 178, 180, 183-184, 187-188, 194-195, 199-200, 202-205, 208-209, 211-212, 217-222, 225, 228, 231-232, 234, 239-240, 248
ghosthunterstore, 228
Ghostly, 163, 224-225, 242
ghostly, 36, 60, 81, 86, 108-109, 119, 149, 160-161, 164-165, 170, 177, 186, 189, 193-194, 207-208, 212-213, 215, 220, 233, 238
ghostlytalk, 225
Ghosts, 5, 11, 23, 41, 49, 71, 81, 96, 114, 123, 130, 138, 145, 162, 211, 217-218, 220, 242-243
ghosts, 7-8, 10-11, 13-14, 18, 23, 31, 35-37, 39, 41, 46, 48, 53-55, 57, 59-60, 62, 67, 81, 84-86, 88-89, 92, 96, 106, 108, 111, 121-122, 127, 135, 142, 145, 147, 150, 160, 163, 165, 167-168, 177, 182-183, 191, 193-194, 198-199, 201-204, 206-207, 209-211, 213-215, 219-221, 223, 230-233, 237, 241
Giles, 219
Gimino, 243
Glen, 228
Glore, 200
glore, 200
Glossary, 6, 229
gnomes, 232
Goln, 35
Goodwin, 225
Gorman, 213
gothic, 214
GPS, 211
Grant, 211, 225
Grave, 200
grave, 78, 248
graves, 129, 185, 191
gravestones, 68, 129
graveyard, 168, 216, 219
graveyards, 36, 79, 81, 85, 127
gravity, 234
gray, 186, 203
grays, 122
great, 14-15, 17, 54, 88, 195, 222, 240
greater, 22
greatgreat, 78
greatly, 106, 174, 185
Greek, 237
Green, 183, 194, 214
Grey, 200
grey, 163
grocery, 179
Groff, 225
guardian, 17, 23
guardians, 17
Guide, 1-3, 5, 7, 9, 11, 13, 15, 17, 19, 21, 23, 25, 27, 29, 31, 33, 35, 37, 39, 41, 43, 45, 47, 49, 51, 53, 55, 57, 59, 61, 63, 65, 67, 69, 71, 73, 75, 77, 79, 81, 83, 85, 87, 89, 91, 93, 95, 97, 99, 101, 103, 105, 107, 109, 111, 113, 115, 117, 119, 121, 123, 125, 127, 129, 131, 133, 135, 137, 139, 141, 143, 145, 147, 149, 151, 153, 155, 157, 159, 161, 163, 165, 167, 169, 171, 173, 175, 177, 179, 181, 183, 185, 187, 189, 191, 193, 195, 197, 199, 201, 203, 205, 207, 209, 211, 213, 215, 217, 219, 221, 223, 225, 227, 229, 231, 233, 235, 237, 239, 241-243, 245, 247
guide, 23, 96, 177-178, 193, 215
Gunter, 220

H

Haining, 242
hair, 16, 109, 131, 145, 156, 158, 161, 174, 176, 194
Hall, 126, 176, 178, 194, 206, 211, 213
Halloween, 113, 127, 136
hallucinates, 89
Hallucinations, 89
hallucinations, 87, 89
handprints, 201
Hannibal, 180
Hans, 224
Hardy, 199
Harper, 243
Harris, 192
Harry, 157, 198
Hat, 38
hat, 9, 37-38, 134-135, 152, 158, 171
Haunt, 131
haunt, 35, 52, 81, 92, 134, 192, 203, 206-207, 218, 220-221, 233
Haunted, 6, 108, 121, 153, 160-161, 169, 197, 199, 214, 221, 226, 242-243, 245, 247
haunted, 36, 48, 80-82, 85, 88, 100, 107, 121, 126, 131, 142, 149, 157, 164, 169, 178, 184, 194, 199-203, 206-209, 211, 213, 216, 218-222, 245-246
hauntedamericatours, 243
hauntedhouses, 165
Haunting, 83, 151, 233, 240
haunting, 35, 39, 43, 49, 57, 62, 88, 90, 106, 150, 159-160, 190-191, 203, 208, 214, 235
Hauntings, 233
hauntings, 18, 87, 233-234
haunts, 136, 186, 205, 217
Hawkins, 211
Hawthorne, 205-206, 219
HearthMasters, 74-75, 166
Heather, 224
heaven, 24
Heavens, 242
heavier, 66
heaviness, 173
heavy, 66, 108, 123, 133, 138, 158-160, 162, 165, 174, 176, 192
Heidi, 133, 242
Heights, 138
heights, 59
Helena, 186
helicopters, 89
hell, 24
Hellhound, 233
Hematite, 101-102
Henderson, 212
Henry, 178, 214, 216, 218
HI, 58
Hickok, 184-185, 191, 195
Hill, 77, 107, 136, 199, 219
hill, 99, 127, 129, 134, 136, 191, 199-200
Hills, 184, 194, 201
HINT, 55, 64, 68, 79, 144, 222
Historic, 184, 198, 207-208, 214
historic, 81, 212
Historical, 90, 147, 173, 217
historical, 195
historicbullock, 203
Hobbs, 223
Hoffman, 43-44, 227
Hole, 241
Hollis, 133, 242
Holzer, 224
Homestake, 194
homicides, 246
Hosey, 211
hospital, 9, 15, 115, 125, 170, 212
Hospitals, 200
hospitals, 82, 215, 221
Hotel, 184-186, 189-191, 194, 202-205, 219-220
hotel, 96, 186-187, 190-191, 202-206, 217-218, 245
Hotels, 202
hotels, 82
hotelsavoy, 203
House, 108, 121, 151-153, 163-164, 169, 191-193, 198-199, 208, 213, 215, 218-219, 242, 245
house, 8-9, 17, 22, 26-27, 29, 31, 36-37, 39, 43, 47, 52, 59, 62, 74, 81-82, 84, 87-90, 96, 98-99, 101, 106, 108-116, 118-119, 121-124, 130-133, 138-140, 142, 144-148, 150-155, 162-165, 167, 169-172, 176, 187, 193, 198-199, 202, 207, 212, 236
Houses, 197, 243
houses, 81, 85, 107, 122, 150, 164, 192, 201, 209, 211, 214
hovering, 31
Howard, 214
Hudgeons, 223-224
Human, 238

human, 19, 27-29, 33, 35, 113-114, 117, 133, 231-233, 237-238, 240
humans, 11-12, 24-25, 41, 240
Hunt, 6
hunt, 33, 54, 63, 76, 92, 97, 125, 188
Hunter, 1-3, 5, 7, 9, 11, 13, 15, 17, 19, 21, 23, 25, 27, 29, 31, 33, 35, 37, 39, 41, 43, 45, 47, 49, 51, 53, 55, 57, 59, 61, 63, 65, 67, 69, 71, 73, 75, 77, 79, 81, 83, 85, 87, 89, 91, 93, 95, 97, 99, 101, 103, 105, 107, 109, 111, 113, 115, 117, 119, 121, 123, 125, 127, 129, 131, 133, 135, 137, 139, 141, 143, 145, 147, 149, 151, 153, 155, 157, 159, 161, 163, 165, 167, 169, 171, 173, 175, 177, 179, 181, 183, 185, 187, 189, 191, 193, 195, 197, 199, 201, 203, 205, 207, 209, 211, 213, 215, 217, 219, 221, 223, 225, 227, 229, 231, 233, 235, 237, 239, 241, 243, 245, 247
hunting, 10, 18, 29, 36, 39, 44, 49, 53-54, 58-59, 63-65, 67-68, 71, 73, 79, 82-83, 88, 90, 93, 97-98, 107, 138, 155, 159, 195, 228, 231, 239
Hyatt, 204
Hypnosis, 48, 51, 227
hypnosis, 7, 48, 53
hypnotist, 19, 48, 240
hypnotists, 53, 227
hypnotized, 51

I

Ian, 223
Icke, 28
Illinois, 199, 207, 212, 219
illuminate, 235
illuminating, 129
Immrama, 44
impaled, 215
Impaler, 215
incarnate, 20, 24
incarnated, 103, 231
Incubus, 234
Independence, 2, 73, 76-77, 80-81, 107-108, 121, 123, 134, 143-145, 148, 156-157, 160, 173, 175, 179-180, 197-200, 212-213, 221, 246-247
Indian, 82, 210, 213
Indians, 210
infamous, 185, 192, 215
infra, 129, 235
Infrared, 13, 94, 227, 235
infrared, 41
Ingleside, 191, 193
inrama, 44
Institute, 227
interdimensional, 232
intruder, 121
intruders, 175
Intuition, 49
intuition, 49
intuitive, 10, 36, 49, 53-54, 235
investigate, 59, 82, 88, 97, 109, 115, 117, 121, 123, 132, 140, 145, 159, 170, 191, 193, 225, 233
investigated, 51, 89, 127, 154, 158, 222, 239
investigating, 30, 35, 226
Investigation, 5, 10, 46, 72-73, 76-77, 83, 90, 93, 107, 228, 246
investigation, 10, 27-28, 36, 50, 57, 59-60, 76, 92-93, 97, 101, 123, 133, 138, 152, 154, 232, 245
investigations, 14, 25, 44, 50, 57, 90, 92, 107, 130, 133, 142, 166, 246
investigative, 49, 157, 180, 224
Investigator, 93-95
investigator, 9, 35, 39, 88, 93-94, 98, 113, 141, 165, 168
Investigators, 93
investigators, 10, 14, 28, 75, 136, 197, 201-202, 216, 226, 232, 246
invisible, 9, 170, 213
ionized, 30, 230
ions, 30
IOPIA, 224
Iowa, 198
IQ, 7
IR, 235
iris, 114
Irish, 35, 126, 204
Iron, 101
iron, 148, 158
ironing, 170
Isaac, 211
Italian, 17, 149
Italianate, 186, 203
Italy, 216

J

Jack, 185
Jackson, 173, 213
Jacob, 202
Jacobean, 176
Jail, 173, 213
jail, 171, 173-175, 179, 219
Jails, 213
jails, 82
Jamaica, 126
James, 77, 107, 136, 147, 170, 173-174, 199, 205, 213, 218, 243
Jamyi, 129, 155-156
Janalea, 43-44, 227
Jane, 177, 185, 191
Janet, 242
Jason, 225, 242
Jasper, 102
Jeff, 224
Jekyll, 205
Jennifer, 110
Jerry, 224
Jesse, 77
Jim, 199, 209
Jimmy, 224
job, 9, 39, 43, 122, 185
jobs, 57, 91
Joe, 136
John, 29, 104, 126, 205, 214-215, 218, 242
Johnny, 185, 191
Johnson, 211
johnZaffis, 29
Jon, 218
Jose, 198
Joseph, 134, 200, 212
Journal, 205
Juan, 220
July, 16-17, 150, 160, 181, 208

K

Kansas, 7, 9, 16, 27, 78, 113, 138, 143, 155, 163, 168, 183, 203-204, 206, 211, 217, 221, 228, 246-247
Kappa, 211
Karl, 47
Kathleen, 37, 242
Kay, 2, 10, 38, 184, 223, 246-247
KCXL, 246
Kent, 78, 138-140
Kentucky, 201, 207, 220
Kevin, 185
KGRA, 223, 246
kgraradio, 223-224, 246
kill, 60
killed, 9, 52, 126, 163, 175, 177, 185, 198, 204, 208, 212-213, 215, 220, 222
killer, 27
killing, 185
kinesis, 237
Kinetic, 234
kinetic, 234
King, 178, 202, 208
Kirk, 242
Kirlian, 234
Kit, 5, 63
Kithcart, 138, 160
Kitty, 194
Klotezke, 223
Kodak, 227
kodak, 227
Kosher, 99
Kris, 225

L

Labradorite, 102
Lakota, 184
Lakotas, 184
Lalaurie, 215
Lancaster, 176
landmarktheatre, 207
Laserthermometers, 227
Latin, 235
Laveau, 200
Lead, 93-94, 195
lead, 83, 104, 143, 209, 236

Leavenworth, 163-165
Lebec, 213
Lecher, 5, 25
Lemp, 201-202
lempmansion, 201
levitated, 188
levitating, 85
Levitation, 234
Lewis, 186, 203
Lexington, 81, 123, 131, 134, 144, 221
Ley, 234, 241, 247
ley, 155, 234
library, 7, 62, 138, 142, 177-178, 226, 229
limestone, 173
Lincoln, 207, 209, 218
Lindsey, 179-182
lions, 216
Lizzie, 202
lizzie, 202
ll, 12, 17-18, 23, 25, 43-44, 46-53, 63, 65, 67, 71, 81, 104, 117, 130, 144
Lombardo, 17, 19, 160
London, 214
Long, 217
Lorin, 223
Lorraine, 104
Louis, 200-201
Louisiana, 200-201, 205, 210, 215
Louisville, 201
Lourdes, 212
loved, 15, 28, 43, 106
Lowery, 224
luck, 10, 50, 66, 81-82, 155
lunatic, 200

M

Mack, 223
Mackey, 207
Madge, 212
Magazine, 246-247
magazine, 8, 50, 247
magic, 102, 105
Magick, 243
magnet, 101
magnetic, 87-88, 234
Magnetometer, 232
Malachite, 102
malice, 145
malicious, 97
Maloney, 223
Mammoth, 220, 242
Manchester, 155
Manhattan, 211
manifest, 43, 64, 90, 235, 240
Manifestation, 234
manifestation, 50, 111, 229
manifestations, 232
manifests, 43, 233
marbles, 64
Marden, 37, 242
Margie, 2, 5, 10, 38, 42, 184, 186, 223, 246-247
margiekay, 223, 228, 245-247
Maria, 4, 148, 247
Marie, 19, 200
Mark, 91, 248
Marshal, 148, 173, 175, 213, 219
Maryland, 209, 212, 220
Mass, 202, 205, 242-243
mass, 20, 185
Massachusetts, 202, 218-219
Massacre, 217, 220
Mastrovich, 192
Materialization, 234
materialize, 59, 133, 136-137, 164
materialized, 33, 129, 187
materializes, 111, 208
materializing, 145
Matrix, 35, 234
matrix, 35
matter, 29-30, 48, 121
MAY, 69
McCall, 185
McClellan, 165
McGee, 204
McLaughlin, 155
Mechanicsville, 211
mediation, 48
meditate, 42, 48, 54, 105
meditated, 127, 150
meditating, 19, 42-44, 114
Meditation, 5, 42, 53, 227
meditation, 42, 44, 51, 90, 149
Meditiation, 227
Medium, 235
medium, 27, 91, 155, 230, 237-238

Mediums, 92, 235
mediums, 23, 27
mediumship, 237
Menger, 220
metal, 68, 160
metallic, 221
metals, 12
metaphysical, 53, 104
Meter, 5, 60, 94
meter, 12, 87-88, 138, 147, 159, 228
Meters, 228
meters, 88
Mexican, 220
Mia, 113, 115-116, 121, 129, 133, 148
Miami, 207
Michael, 78, 138, 140
Middleton, 224
Midlothian, 199
Midnight, 185
midnight, 127
Military, 208-209
military, 90, 154
Miller, 217
minerals, 65, 67, 232
miscarriages, 87
Mississippi, 191, 205
Missouri, 2, 17, 36, 76-77, 80-81, 107-108, 138, 155, 157, 169, 174, 179-181, 197, 199-201, 203-204, 206, 210-213, 217, 221, 242, 246
Mist, 84, 235
mist, 50, 72, 111, 113, 136, 140, 152, 159, 211, 235
mists, 210
misty, 33, 36, 199
MO, 77-78, 134, 173, 199-200, 203, 210, 217, 221
Moaning, 220
moaning, 27
molecules, 30
Mollie, 78
Monocular, 59
monocular, 59, 63
Monoculars, 227
Monoxide, 109
monoxide, 140
monsters, 132
Montana, 186, 203, 209
Montego, 126
Montgomery, 157
Moon, 93
moon, 129
moonlight, 93, 115
moonlit, 127
Moore, 198
Moriah, 191
morphing, 111
mosthaunted, 226
Mound, 127, 200
Mount, 134, 191
Mountain, 209
mountains, 215
Muddiman, 242
MUFON, 223-224
Murder, 85, 198
murder, 27, 172
murdered, 27, 52, 126, 184-185, 219
murderer, 174, 198
murderers, 184
murders, 202
Muse, 194
Museum, 173, 191-194, 200, 202, 219
museum, 165, 174, 193-194, 199
Myrtles, 201, 205
Myrtlesplantation, 205
Mysteries, 186
mysteries, 182
mysterious, 9, 214
mysteriously, 133, 136
Mystery, 198
Mystical, 229, 243

N

Nancy, 30, 242
Nash, 217
Nathan, 192
Nathaniel, 206
National, 184, 198, 207-209, 214, 220
national, 246
Native, 17, 26-27, 122, 133
native, 81, 186, 246
natural, 27, 54, 66, 88, 202, 220, 231, 239, 246
Naturally, 108, 179, 183
naturally, 14
NDE, 235
NE, 216
Negative, 5, 101, 103-104

negative, 27-29, 38-39, 44-46, 64, 96-98, 100-102, 104, 106, 111, 122, 132, 167, 174, 192, 232, 234, 236
negativity, 66, 97-98, 101-102, 111
Netherlands, 30
newcaslte, 216
Newcastle, 216
News, 223, 226, 246-247
NewspaperArchive, 226
newspapers, 90, 92, 246
Nigh, 94
Night, 5, 59, 63, 93, 127, 235
nightmares, 39
Nightsearch, 224
nightsearch, 224
nightvisionbinoculars, 227
Nightwatch, 224
Nightwatchers, 224
nightwatchradio, 224
Nikon, 118
Nocturna, 2
NocturnaPress, 2
Noland, 200
NonPhysical, 25
Noory, 223
Northumberland, 216
NY, 204, 207

OBE, 236
obituaries, 156
obituary, 90
object, 64, 68, 91, 140, 147, 149, 229, 234-235, 237, 240
objects, 5, 26-27, 29, 36, 46, 58, 64-65, 85-87, 105, 150, 160, 198, 206, 230, 235-240, 246
Obsidian, 101-102
obsidian, 98, 101
Occult, 207
odor, 84
Offutt, 242
Oglethorpe, 209
Oklahoma, 207
omen, 230
ominous, 148, 150
Opera, 208
Orb, 84, 235
orb, 29, 33, 36, 76-77, 141, 162-163, 189
Orbs, 5, 29, 72, 235-236
orbs, 11, 20-21, 29-31, 33, 50, 58, 72, 75, 106, 129, 136-137, 140-142, 162, 169, 177, 188-189, 209, 211, 240
Order, 214
Orleans, 200, 215
Osage, 157, 210
Oscar, 207
Ouija, 54, 96, 236
Oxford, 242
Oyster, 191
oysters, 191
ozarkmt, 53, 227

P

PA, 208, 210, 214
Palmer, 126
Pam, 185
Paracast, 225
Paracon, 246
Paralysis, 238
Paranormal, 6, 36, 93, 202, 222-226, 229, 236-237, 243, 247
paranormal, 7, 14, 31, 36, 39, 53-54, 75, 84-85, 108-109, 113, 123, 125, 132-133, 150, 154-155, 157, 159-160, 162-163, 168, 188, 197, 199, 202, 204, 213, 216, 223-226, 232, 236, 246
Parapsychology, 236
ParaSpiritual, 224
Paris, 215
Parish, 205
Park, 72-73, 76-77, 107, 134, 136, 199, 202, 208-209, 219-220
park, 72-73, 76-77, 129, 134-137, 156, 180-181, 199, 220-221
particles, 177
passenger, 130
passengers, 217
Pearl, 102, 115, 151-153
Pemberton, 213
pendant, 66
Pendulum, 66

pendulum, 5, 48, 60, 65-68, 90, 97-98, 100, 138, 180, 232
Pendulums, 5, 60, 228
pendulums, 66
Penitentiary, 213
Pennsylvania, 208, 210, 213
Perception, 8, 233
perception, 50, 237, 239
perceptions, 12
Perfume, 84
perfume, 194
Peridot, 102
perished, 211, 218
persecution, 216
Pershing, 217
Peter, 121-122, 242
petroglyphs, 33
pets, 42, 59, 91
phantasm, 236
Phantom, 236
phantom, 238
phantoms, 207
Phenomena, 60
phenomena, 26, 87, 158-159, 199, 231, 233, 236, 238-239
Phenomenon, 232, 237
phenomenon, 26
Philadelphia, 214
photograph, 31, 76, 78, 162
photographic, 37, 41, 57, 234
Photographing, 5, 71, 162
photographing, 41
photographs, 29, 72, 78, 118, 140, 162, 187, 209
photons, 20, 23, 29, 106
Photos, 5, 166
Physical, 5
physical, 12, 20-21, 25, 33, 45, 50, 96, 106, 216, 229-230, 233, 236-237, 240
physically, 17, 21, 45, 49, 85-86, 183
physicist, 37
physics, 168
Pi, 211
pi, 242
Pierpont, 217
Pike, 210
Place, 61, 64, 201
Places, 5, 81, 198, 207-208, 214
places, 48, 81-82, 132, 140, 142, 152, 159, 181, 183, 202, 230
plague, 216
planchette, 236
Planet, 225
planet, 21, 24, 35
planets, 20, 24
Plantation, 126, 201, 205
plantation, 126, 201
Plasma, 5, 30
plasma, 30-31, 230
Plymouth, 210, 219
poison, 52
poisoned, 52
Polaroid, 72
Police, 180
police, 110, 115, 155, 160, 171, 179, 182, 226
Poltergeist, 5, 26, 236
poltergeist, 27-28, 30, 98, 121, 204, 229, 243
Poltergeists, 26
poltergeists, 11
Pope, 121
Portal, 112, 237
portal, 112-114, 117, 122, 150, 166, 241
portals, 161, 236
Porter, 179-182
Porterfield, 198
possess, 233
Possession, 92, 237
possession, 28-29, 92, 146, 231, 237
possessions, 28, 102
Powerball, 53
powers, 106
Praagh, 243
Pranks, 90
pranks, 82, 159
prankster, 109, 154, 221
precognition, 233
predict, 246
pregnant, 121, 174, 192, 207
premises, 194
Presbyterian, 134
presence, 8, 23, 28, 48, 57, 60, 76, 81, 87, 91, 108, 111, 115, 121, 123, 129, 131, 133, 138, 140, 146-147, 149, 159, 161, 170, 173-176, 187-188, 192-194, 205, 210, 231
presences, 206
President, 209, 218
president, 205
Prisons, 213
prisons, 82
Projection, 230
projection, 229, 236

proof, 18, 54, 71, 245
Prospect, 204
prospector, 72, 135
prospectors, 184
Protect, 5, 97
protect, 9, 28-29, 39, 97-98, 100, 111, 122, 176
protected, 26, 104
protecting, 122
Protection, 102
protection, 11, 28, 39, 63, 66, 90, 97-102, 229
Protective, 82, 102
protective, 97, 101
protector, 27, 102
PsiTalk, 224
psitalk, 224
Psychiatric, 200
Psychic, 54, 89, 102, 237, 243-244
psychic, 7, 9, 14, 25, 34, 36, 41-42, 45-47, 49, 51, 53-55, 85, 89, 97, 100, 104, 106, 111, 113, 124, 135, 165, 177, 179, 228, 231, 235, 239, 244, 246
psychically, 45, 148
Psychics, 5, 12-13, 62
psychics, 14, 27, 62, 89-90, 107, 193, 234, 239-240
Psychokinesis, 237
psychological, 45
Psychologist, 47
Psychology, 240
Psychometry, 237
Punnett, 223

Q

Quantrill, 213
Quartz, 98, 102
quartz, 66, 98, 100
Queen, 192, 200, 217-218
QUEST, 10, 46, 76-77, 107, 147, 155, 219, 228, 246
Quest, 10, 72-73, 228

R

Race, 223
Rachel, 129, 147-148
Radio, 6, 13, 223-225, 237, 246
radio, 12, 62, 164, 170, 223-225, 237, 241, 246
Railroad, 205, 220
railroad, 82, 123, 125, 143-144, 168, 179-181, 205, 217, 220
railway, 217
Rainbow, 101
Raleigh, 214
Ralston, 77, 107, 136
Record, 229
record, 14, 26, 35, 47, 51, 93
recorded, 25
Recorder, 60
recorder, 51, 60-61, 86, 91, 101, 138, 142, 154, 232
Regency, 204
Register, 184, 207-208, 214
Registry, 198
reincarnate, 24
Reincarnation, 242
reincarnation, 24
Rener, 8
Rense, 224
reptile, 221
Reptilian, 28
reptilian, 28
Research, 30, 224-225, 242
researcher, 18, 30, 92, 159
researchers, 33, 36, 39, 112, 223, 246
researching, 53
Resources, 6, 48, 226-227
Restaurant, 191, 201, 221
Restaurants, 202
Retrocognition, 237
retrocognition, 233
Revolutionary, 226
Reynolds, 212
Rhine, 47, 236
Rhythmic, 227
Riccio, 243
Richard, 223
Richetti, 217
Richmond, 211
ritual, 233
rituals, 207

River, 180-181, 200, 202, 205
Riverstone, 102
Riverview, 205
Robert, 213, 242
Robinson, 199
Rochereau, 215
rod, 5, 64, 67, 114
Rods, 5, 60, 67
rods, 11, 46, 60, 65, 67-68, 155, 228, 232
Romania, 215
Rome, 216
Ron, 99
Room, 204, 217
room, 9, 12, 17, 26-27, 37-39, 50, 58-59, 82, 91, 105, 108-111, 113, 115, 118, 121, 123, 132, 138, 140, 142, 147-150, 153-155, 163-164, 170-172, 174, 177-178, 186-188, 193, 198, 202, 205-206, 213, 217, 223
Rooms, 206
Roosevelt, 186-187
Rosa, 126
Rose, 126
Rotary, 72-73, 76-77, 134, 136
Route, 207
Rowman, 242
Royal, 215
Royce, 223
Ruby, 101-102
Rudzik, 136
Rule, 83, 87
RVP, 237
Ryan, 225

S

Sabrina, 191
Sagamore, 204
Saint, 205, 212, 220
Salem, 205-206, 218
Salina, 207
Saloon, 191, 194
Sam, 179
Samuel, 205
San, 198-199, 209, 213, 220
Sanatorium, 201
sanatorium, 201
Sanderson, 242
Sara, 130-131
Sarah, 130, 198, 211
saucer, 150
Saucers, 37
Savoy, 203
Schnellgeister, 221
School, 212-213
Schools, 211
Schrader, 224
Science, 37, 242
scientific, 10, 54, 57, 236
scientists, 12, 30, 87
Scotland, 176, 215-216
Scott, 143-144, 225
Scout, 108
scratching, 88, 123
scream, 170
screamed, 163
screaming, 9, 109, 164, 171
screams, 216
screen, 177
Séance, 237
séance, 230, 232, 239
séances, 235
Second, 2, 202
seconds, 31, 76, 105, 118, 136, 222
Secret, 28, 133, 242
secret, 187
Security, 152, 154
seeing, 7, 25-26, 38, 46, 48-49, 55, 89, 132, 152, 170, 182, 206, 209, 215-216, 222, 231, 238
seekers, 184
Sense, 5, 49, 233
sense, 10-11, 14-15, 17, 38, 48-49, 58, 71, 85, 101, 103, 113, 122-123, 131, 140, 174, 231, 237, 240
sensed, 27, 31, 72-73, 76, 108, 117, 133, 138, 146-148, 187, 194, 203, 236
senses, 49, 233, 239
sensitive, 9
sensor, 153
sensors, 152
Sensory, 8, 233
sensory, 237, 239
sequence, 14
Seth, 185-187, 191, 203
Seton, 212
settlers, 122, 210
Seven, 219
Seymour, 177

Shadow, 5, 37, 133, 238, 242, 244
shadow, 18, 37-39, 123-124, 128-129, 150, 183, 194, 222, 244
Shadows, 243
shadows, 50, 58, 132, 210, 220, 242-243
shaman, 17
Shape, 238
shapeless, 150
Sharpsburg, 209
Sheets, 224
Sheila, 225
Sheraton, 220
Sherman, 194
Shifting, 238
Shining, 202
Shows, 6, 223, 225
Sibley, 210
Sightings, 39, 224
sightings, 30, 36, 39, 84-85, 89, 150, 191, 201, 204, 210, 224
sign, 15, 51, 134
signs, 88-89
Simulacra, 238
sinister, 105, 174
Sir, 214
Sirona, 243
sis, 69
sister, 7, 16, 76, 79, 115, 170, 172, 179
Site, 93, 194, 204, 217-218, 220
sixteen, 7
Sixth, 5, 49, 233
sixth, 10, 14, 49, 219
skeletal, 191
skeptic, 87
skeptics, 54
Skizz, 225
slave, 126
slavery, 10
slaves, 126, 215
Smells, 84
Smith, 134
smoke, 45, 140, 143-144, 168, 187-188, 219
smoker, 188
smoking, 187-188
Smoky, 102
Snallygaster, 221
solders, 211
Soldier, 211
soldier, 221
soldiers, 81, 107, 125, 199, 208-210, 213
soul, 20-21, 23-24, 38, 118
souls, 217
sound, 9, 11-12, 88, 96, 98, 115, 117, 147, 160, 170, 248
sounded, 115, 117, 174
Source, 244
Sources, 88-89
species, 194
specific, 58, 231, 240
Specter, 238
spectral, 214
Spectrum, 13
spectrum, 12-13, 162, 232
Spencer, 205
Spirit, 5, 31-32, 235-236, 238, 240
spirit, 11-12, 15, 17-25, 27-29, 31, 33, 41, 43, 49-50, 52-54, 58, 60, 64, 71, 74, 81, 87, 91-92, 96, 101, 106, 109, 111, 121, 124, 128, 140, 145-147, 152, 156, 158-160, 165, 167, 174, 177, 182-183, 191, 193, 199, 203, 214, 229-230, 232-237, 240
Spirited, 242
Spirits, 5, 12, 19, 23-24, 33, 35, 41, 65, 131, 238, 240, 243
spirits, 8-11, 18-19, 24, 26, 28-31, 33-35, 37, 39, 41, 46, 48-50, 52-54, 59, 62, 64, 71-72, 81-82, 86, 89, 91-92, 96-97, 99-100, 102-104, 106-107, 111-112, 122, 125, 129, 131, 133, 135, 137, 140, 142, 145, 147, 149-150, 152, 155, 159, 161, 163, 166, 168, 170, 173, 176-177, 187, 194, 201, 203, 210, 214, 216, 219-221, 230, 232-233, 235-237, 240, 243, 246
spiritual, 31, 33, 45, 234
Spiritualism, 238
Spring, 34, 134, 185
Springfield, 16, 169, 206
Springs, 204
Sprite, 240
Sprites, 5, 33-34
sprites, 30, 34-35, 137, 232, 240
Square, 47, 81, 157, 175
stabbing, 171
stage, 44, 49, 192
staircase, 108, 113
stairway, 189, 199
stand, 29, 46, 50, 62, 78, 98, 132
Stanley, 202-203
stanleyhotel, 202
Stanton, 37, 242
Staph, 15
Star, 185-186, 203

Stephen, 202
Stephens, 211
Sterling, 81, 134
Steve, 223-224
Stewart, 242
Stigmata, 238
Stones, 102
Strange, 224
strange, 11, 34, 36-37, 50, 82, 87, 116, 154, 162, 164, 186, 188, 207, 209, 211, 221
stream, 72, 74, 79, 135, 168, 187
Stroud, 213
Stuart, 207
Students, 212
subconscious, 44-45, 48, 64-65, 67, 240
Succubus, 239
Suffolk, 242
Supernatural, 239
supernatural, 96
Sutherland, 156
Sutton, 214
Swearengen, 185, 192
Swiss, 47
SyFy, 225-226
Syracuse, 207

T

tactile, 57
Takoo, 126
Talbott, 30
Tamie, 152
Taneytown, 208
TAPS, 225
Target, 239
Taylor, 243
TB, 201
Team, 30, 147
Tech, 228
tech, 57, 164, 228
Technical, 246
technician, 116, 155
technique, 46, 48, 50, 62, 133
Techniques, 5, 57
techniques, 28, 48-49, 53-55, 82, 104, 122
Teddy, 187
teenage, 113
teenager, 26, 90
teenagers, 26
Teens, 26
teens, 92
teepees, 125
teeth, 26, 221
Telekinesis, 234, 237, 239
telepathic, 34, 60, 101, 182
telepathically, 7, 17, 19, 34-35, 138, 180-181, 240
Telepathy, 239
telepathy, 8, 46, 53, 233
teleports, 229
television, 62, 87, 177, 223, 241
Temperature, 93
temperature, 58, 85, 136, 165, 168
Tennessee, 209, 214, 224
tennis, 64
Terms, 6, 229
Texas, 209, 220, 224
Theater, 206-207
theater, 207-208
theatre, 192, 202, 206-208
Theatres, 206
Theoretical, 234
theoretical, 241
theory, 14, 33, 162, 166, 177, 237, 241
theparacast, 225
Therapy, 247
Thermometer, 5, 57-58, 93
Thermometers, 227
Theta, 42
Thomas, 78, 214
Thurnam, 178
Thurnham, 176
Time, 5, 14, 25-26, 50, 93, 135, 159, 240
time, 7-9, 11-12, 14-17, 20-26, 28-29, 31, 33, 37, 41-43, 46-51, 53-54, 57, 59-60, 62, 67, 71, 73-74, 78, 81, 83, 85, 89, 91, 93, 96-99, 104, 106, 108, 110-112, 115-116, 118, 121, 123, 125, 127, 129, 131, 136, 138, 142-143, 145, 147, 149-150, 152, 157, 159-160, 162, 165, 169-170, 176-177, 179-182, 187, 191, 215, 230, 232, 237, 240-241, 246
Tina, 179, 182
Tipping, 239
Todd, 224
Tombstone, 219
tombstone, 128
Tongues, 238

Tony, 224
Tools, 5, 57
Toumaline, 102
Tourmaline, 101
Tower, 214
tragic, 207
trailer, 156
train, 44, 52, 89, 143-144, 208, 220
Trains, 143
trains, 42, 143
Trance, 146, 148, 240
trance, 19, 21-23, 27-28, 35, 44, 51, 91, 121, 123-125, 135, 146, 148, 152, 154-155, 179-181, 183, 229, 238
Transcendental, 53
Transformation, 227
transition, 23
translucent, 229
transparent, 36, 83, 144, 149, 152, 233
Transylvania, 215
Tree, 5, 33-35, 77, 137, 240
tree, 34-35, 77, 89, 118, 127, 132, 135-137, 240
Trees, 35
trees, 7, 33, 35, 118, 133, 137, 208, 240
Trillium, 205
Troy, 243
Truman, 157, 197-198, 242
Try, 12, 42, 47, 62, 67
tsunami, 53
tubes, 232
Turquoise, 102
Twain, 248
Tyne, 216
Typhoid, 192

U

UFO, 7-8, 28, 30, 36, 59-60, 66, 84-85, 150, 204, 223-224, 240, 247
ufo, 242
UFOs, 7, 37, 41, 150
UK, 225
uk, 28, 214, 216, 226
Ultra, 162
Ultraviolet, 13
Ulysses, 211
Unexplained, 189, 225-226, 239-240
unexplained, 36, 188, 191, 194, 206, 219, 222, 238
Unidentified, 73, 240
Union, 81, 175, 217
United, 199, 201
Universe, 24
universe, 234
University, 47, 211-212, 242
Unsolved, 186
unsolved, 246
USO, 241
UV, 5, 60

V

Vaile, 80
Valentine, 220
Valley, 210
vegetarian, 41, 45
veil, 159
vents, 62, 88, 91, 232
Vibratory, 5
vibratory, 12, 24, 41, 45
Victoria, 158
Victorian, 81, 138, 171, 186, 192, 202-203, 208
Viewing, 50
viewing, 53, 92, 133, 237, 246
Villisca, 198
villiscaiowa, 198
Violet, 162, 199
Virgil, 219
Virginia, 211
Visible, 13
visible, 12, 30, 33-34, 74, 78-79, 114, 129, 137, 152, 189, 229, 233-236, 240
Vision, 5, 59, 63, 94, 235
vision, 16, 34, 46, 59, 63, 93, 172, 188, 190, 203, 235, 240
visions, 21, 176
visitation, 240
visited, 110, 124, 126, 147, 173, 181, 197, 200, 205, 220
visiting, 50, 108, 127, 134, 152, 193, 199, 203, 214, 217, 219
Visitor, 194
Visitors, 194, 198, 209-211, 215-216, 219

visitors, 81, 150, 175, 185, 191, 193, 198, 201, 209-210, 212-213, 216
visualization, 98
Visualize, 43
visualize, 43, 46, 64, 96-97, 100
visualizing, 97
volt, 12
voltage, 234
volts, 12
Voodoo, 200
voodoo, 126
Vortex, 31, 241
vortex, 155

W

Wallace, 157, 198
Wallachia, 215
Walnut, 78, 206
Walter, 214
Waning, 93
Ward, 203, 219
Wards, 157
Warren, 104
Warrensburg, 211
Washington, 210, 218
Watkins, 234
wavelength, 235
wavelengths, 235
Waverly, 201
waves, 12, 42
Waxing, 93
Whaley, 199
Wheeler, 211
Whispering, 84
whistle, 52
Whitmore, 242
Wichita, 143
Wikipedia, 243
Wilder, 207
Will, 191
William, 194, 202, 210, 213-214
Willie, 214
Wilson, 218
Winchester, 198
Wind, 5, 60, 62, 228
windmeter, 228
Windtronic, 228
Winkowski, 243
Witch, 126, 214-215, 220
witch, 105, 218
witchcraft, 126
Witches, 228
witches, 105, 219
witching, 65
Witness, 223
Woodlawn, 200
woods, 31, 181
wormhole, 241
WWII, 217

Y

Yankee, 199
Yeater, 211
YMCA, 219
York, 204, 207, 242
Yvette, 226

Z

Zac, 225
Zaffis, 29, 104
Zener, 47-48
Ziganshin, 36
zigzag, 32
Zircon, 102
Zizzi, 149